ORIGINS

L. James Gibson

Pacific Press® Publishing Association
Nampa, Idaho
Oshawa, Ontario, Canada
www.pacificpress.com

Cover design by Gerald Lee Monks
Cover design resources from Lars Justinen
Inside design by Kristin Hansen-Mellish

Copyright © 2012 by Pacific Press® Publishing Association
Printed in the United States of America
All rights reserved

The author assumes full responsibility for the accuracy of all facts and quotations as cited in this book.

You can obtain additional copies of this book by calling toll-free 1-800-765-6955 or by visiting http://www.adventistbookcenter.com.

ISBN 13: 978-0-8163-3788-0
ISBN 10: 0-8163-3788-8

12 13 14 15 16 • 5 4 3 2 1

Dedication

To Dottie

"A good wife is her husband's pride and joy."
—Proverbs 12:4

Table of Contents

Introduction

The first three chapters of Genesis provide the context in which the rest of Scripture finds its meaning. These chapters show us the identity of the only true God, and the origin of our world and of the diverse species with which we share the planet. They reveal the privileges and responsibilities with which we were created, the meaning of our existence, and how sin and death first entered our world. They expose the battle going on between good and evil, and provide the first hints of God's plan to defeat the evil one and restore us to Him. These three chapters are crucial for our understanding of God, ourselves, and our world.

One purpose of this book is to encourage the reader to review the biblical teaching about origins carefully. Even when read superficially, Genesis 1–3 is a fascinating history of Creation and the Fall. There are important issues here: creation of an unspoiled world without violence or death; creation by command (fiat) in six days; special creation of humans in God's image. These are basic facts of biblical teaching, and denying their importance exposes one to spiritual danger. But these chapters contain much more.

A second purpose is to show how the doctrine of a six-day Creation affects all aspects of our Christian view of life. In the Creation story, we find the meaning of marriage and family, of responsibility and work, and of Sabbath rest. In the story of the Fall, we discover how we and our world became estranged from God, a condition that has brought suffering and death—but also the promise that the serpent, the originator of evil, would eventually be crushed. It is what Genesis 3 tells us about the Fall that enables us to understand our need of a Savior and the reason for our dependence on God's grace. The gospel story is grounded in the events of Genesis 1–3.

A third purpose in writing is to warn against the effects of diluting the biblical teaching of Creation and the Fall. It has become quite fashionable in some circles to deny creation without violence and death, creation in six days, special creation of humans, and much more. Even within the church, we hear voices of disbelief calling us to "grow up" and move beyond the biblical teaching. This shouldn't surprise us; we've been warned that in the end time, major conflicts will erupt over Creation and the gospel.[1] In view of the importance of these issues, it is vital that we each are informed regarding them and their implications.

Many people have helped with the development of the ideas in this book. Ronny Nalin, Raul Esperante, Tim Standish, Kathy Ching, Ariel Roth, Humberto Rasi, Richard Davidson, Gerhard Pfandl, and Nancy and Gerald Vyhmeister each reviewed one or more chapters, and many other colleagues, too numerous to mention, have contributed to my understanding through conferences and conversations. It's unlikely that any of these people agree with everything I've written here, but their comments and suggestions were important, and I appreciate them. Naturally, any remaining mistakes are my own responsibility.

In addition, I thank my wife, Dottie, for her patience and understanding while I focused my attention on this work. I also thank the two and the twelve for all they have taught me.

1. Revelation 14:6–12; see also White, EG. *Evangelism*. Washington, DC: Review and Herald® Publishing Association (1946), 593, 594.

CHAPTER 1

God and the Universe

"In the beginning God . . ." These words, the first in the Bible, state that God was present at the beginning of creation. God Himself doesn't have a beginning—He is eternal. Although we struggle to understand what that means, the conclusion is inescapable (see Romans 1:20). Tracing back through history, we find a chain of causes and effects until we reach the beginning of everything. At this point there are no physical causes—if no universe exists, then there's nothing physical that could be the first cause. We must postulate, then, that at the beginning of existence, there was an eternal, uncaused cause. That cause is God.[1]

Someone might argue that the universe is eternal and so doesn't need a cause—and thus there is no need to postulate a Creator. But the universe cannot be eternal.[2] If it were eternal, everything in it that could break down would have broken down below the level of individual atoms, reaching maximum disorder ("heat death"), and life could not survive in a universe in that state. But the universe has a great deal of order and shows evidence of having a beginning. Thus one cannot reasonably claim that the universe is eternal. We must conclude, instead, that there was a beginning, and that God existed before the universe came into being. God was at the beginning. This conclusion holds true regardless of when the universe was created.

God *created*

Bara, the Hebrew word translated as "created," is used only for actions done by God, although not always in the sense of *ex nihilo* (out of nothing). In addition to its being used in Genesis 1:1 of the entire work of creation, it is used of the creation of great sea creatures (Genesis 1:21), of humans (Genesis 1:27; 5:1, 2), and of the creating in general that God did during Creation week (Genesis 2:3). We can understand it here as referring to an event beyond human ability.

The universe was not made of preexisting material; it was created from nothing (*ex nihilo*) by the word of God.[3] Of course, God *had* to create the universe from nothing because before He created the universe, nothing existed that He could have formed to make the universe. Genesis 1:1 portrays the absolute sovereignty of God. He speaks and it is done (Psalm 33:9; Genesis 1:3ff.).

Scripture also portrays God's creating as a peaceful process; God doesn't have to struggle with difficult matter or with other gods. This negates the view of some critical scholars that Genesis is merely a Hebrew version of an ancient creation myth like those of other Near Eastern cultures. No, the Creation story in Genesis is fundamentally different from the creation stories of the surrounding cultures.[4] Besides the lack of conflict and violence in the creation portrayed in Scripture, the scriptural account differs from those other creation stories in that it pictures God as preexisting and having absolute sovereignty, and it portrays Him as valuing humans highly.

The heavens and the earth

There are different opinions regarding the scope of the Genesis creation—regarding how much of the universe the phrase "the heavens and the earth" refers to. Three major views have been proposed:[5] that the phrase refers to the entire universe; that it refers to our solar system; or that it refers to planet Earth's ecosphere.

Proponents of the first view point to *merisms:* literary constructions in which a phrase uses opposites, such as "day and night," to indicate totality ("all the time"). If "the heavens and the earth" is a merism, then Genesis 1:1 is referring to the creation of the entire universe. This could be called the "universal creation" interpretation. Some people have postulated a gap in time between the creation of the universe in verse 1 and the beginning of the six-day Creation in verse 3.[6] This is known as the "passive gap" theory.

A second view is that "the heavens and the earth" refers to our solar system, not the entire universe. The ancients had no concept of the difference between a solar system and the universe, and the Hebrew language doesn't have a word that expresses that distinction. Thus, they might have used the ordinary words for "heavens" (*shamayim*) and "earth" (*'eretz*) to describe the creation of the solar system. God could have created the rest of the universe other than our solar system before Creation week, then created our earth and solar system at the beginning of that week, or during it, then prepared the earth for living things, and then populated the earth with those living things during Creation week. This view could be called the "solar system creation" interpretation. In this case, we might not interpret Genesis 1:1 as referring to creation of the universe from nothing, while pointing out that other texts do affirm creation of the universe *ex nihilo*.[7]

A third interpretation is that the term "the heavens and the earth" refers to our earth's ecosphere.[8] Proponents of this view say our planet could have been in a lifeless state, much like Venus or Mars, for an undetermined length of time prior to Creation week. Then, during Creation week, God transformed a previously uninhabitable planet Earth into an organized and inhabited world. We can call this the "ecosphere creation" interpretation.

Other textual evidence can help us to determine whether the entire universe was created at the same time as our world, or whether other parts of the universe might have existed before Creation week. Note, for instance, Job 38:4–7. It speaks of "sons of God" rejoicing when God created our world. Obviously, they had been created before Creation week. And the presence of Satan in the Garden of Eden (in the form of a serpent) implies a prior history of rebellion and fall (Isaiah 14; Ezekiel 28), as does the "great controversy" metanarrative, which posits the existence and fall of Lucifer before the creation of Adam and Eve.[9] In addition, there is no record of when the water was created. It is already present when the Creation story begins (Genesis 1:2; 2 Peter 3:5).

Regardless of which interpretation we consider to be the best, the Bible is clear that God is the Creator of the entire universe and of our world and its inhabitants, and that He created it all from nothing by the power of His word.

The heavens declare

We can tell something about builders by the design and quality of the buildings they construct. Of course, one needs to know the purpose for which the building was intended: we wouldn't expect an office building to look like a church or a house to look like a grocery store. Various factors determine the design of a building: among them, the way the building will be used, our esthetics and resources, and other factors, such as climate and topography. We may be able to infer some of these constraints by examining the design and function of the building. Similarly, we can make inferences regarding the Builder of the universe when we examine its structure and design.[10]

First, we see a universe that is vast. From our perspective, it seems infinite—it extends beyond our ability to see either directly or using our most sophisticated technology. Nor can we measure the tremendous amounts of matter and energy in the universe. The size of the universe implies that the Creator's power and abilities are unlimited.

Second, we see order in the universe. Matter is arranged in interesting groupings, forming such things as spiral galaxies and black holes. Matter and energy interact in regular patterns that we can describe using mathematical equations. This, in itself, is truly remarkable, and it argues for a purposeful creation. There is no other reason that the universe should have such mathematical properties. The order in the universe also tells us something important. All the physical systems we observe tend to become more disorderly over time. This is considered to be one of the laws of nature. The orderliness of our universe shows it was created with order and is not eternal. If it were eternal, it would now be completely disordered.

Observation of the universe also tells us that it has the properties necessary to support life. This cannot be attributed to chance; it must be the result of intelligent planning. We can demonstrate this with a thought experiment.

Imagine that you were given the task of designing a universe where life could exist and thrive. Picture yourself in front of a wall on which there are fifty dials that control the physical properties of the universe. Your job is to choose a value for each physical property and set each dial accordingly. For example, you must determine how strong the force of gravitational attraction between objects should be, and what properties the fundamental particles that comprise matter should have. You must decide how much mass and electrical charge each particle should have, and how the particles should be held together to form atoms, and how strong the nuclear forces should be. To find the right combination of values for all fifty dials simultaneously would be a daunting task indeed.

However, the problem is much more difficult than even those fifty dials might suggest. Scientists say the universe is finely tuned. They have found that if life is to exist, the values for the various physical properties of the universe must be set at very precise levels. The slightest error would produce a universe very different from the one we inhabit. The possibility of all those dials being set just where they would have to be for life to exist is too small to support the idea that it could have happened by chance.

God was completely free to create any kind of universe He wanted. He could have chosen any number of combinations of different values for the various physical laws and forces, depending on His purpose for the universe. The fitness of our universe for life cannot be the result of chance. It is the result of intelligent planning. The fine-tuning of the physical constants tells us that the Creator is infinitely intelligent and that He intended for life to exist.

The vastness and order of the universe, together with its being precisely formed so as to be fit for life, is powerfully consistent with the biblical revelation of the Creator God. He created freely, with unlimited power, wisdom, and resources. He is consistent and rules by laws of His own choosing, which means that we would expect the universe to have both regularities that we can discover through systematic study and singularities beyond the reach of our minds or other resources. Truly, the heavens do declare the glory of God (Psalm 19:1).

Big bang theory

Scientists have tried to explain the origin and structure of the universe by studying its features. This brings a dilemma. Scientists used to include God in their explanations, but this is no longer considered acceptable. As currently practiced, science is strictly naturalistic—which means it excludes any discussion of God or supernatural causes. To be considered scientific, an explanation for the origin of the universe must refer only to physical processes. This means that if the universe actually was created by a supernatural act, science would never know it—its philosophy precludes it from ever knowing the truth.

The current scientific theory of the origin of the universe is known as the big bang theory.[11] This theory recognizes that the universe had a beginning, but it doesn't explain what caused the beginning. Rather, it assumes a beginning and tries to use the known physical laws to explain the present structure of the universe. Nevertheless, the question of the origin of the universe continues to be important.

The idea that the universe had a beginning raises challenging questions for naturalistic scientists. For people who deny the existence of God, it is philosophically preferable to suppose that the universe is eternal, because there is no need to explain the origin of something that is eternal. Because of this philosophical bias, naturalistic scientists experienced considerable discomfort when evidence was discovered that suggested the universe had a beginning and isn't eternal. That evidence came from observations made by astronomer Edwin Hubble in 1929.

Hubble noted that stars in different parts of the universe produce light of slightly different colors and that some of the light seemed "redshifted"; that is, the wavelength of that light was longer, and the greater the distance from the earth, the greater the shift in the wavelength. (Red light has a longer wavelength than do the other colors of light.) The explanation for this "red shift" seemed to be that the stars were moving away from the earth rapidly enough that the light waves from distant stars were taking longer to reach the earth, causing them to be redder. And the more distant galaxies seemed to be moving away from earth faster than the nearer ones. All this led to the idea that the stars must be moving apart, which implies that they were closer together in the past than they are now.

If the stars used to be closer together than they are now, then, if you go far enough back in time, you must reach a time when all of the stars were crowded together. In fact, scientists have concluded that there must have been a time when all the stars were joined together in a single point of unimaginable energy. They believe that not only the stars, but time and space also must have been contained in that single point. The point, then, expanded rapidly, causing time to begin and, in a process that has occupied about thirteen to fourteen billion years, forming the stars and galaxies that we see today. This theory cannot be true unless the universe had a beginning.

At first, scientists with a naturalistic viewpoint opposed the idea that the universe had a beginning. One of them, British astronomer Sir Fred Hoyle, derisively called the theory the "big bang." The name stuck, and we still refer to the theory as the "big bang theory."

This theory stimulated new ideas, one of them being that if the big bang was true, there should be some heat from the big bang still present throughout the universe, and it should be uniformly distributed in all parts of the universe. In 1964, scientists did indeed discover "cosmic microwave background radiation," which fit the specifications of the theory. This discovery led to general acceptance of the big bang theory by scientists.

The big bang theory also explains the abundance of elements in the universe—for example, explaining why hydrogen and helium are very abundant while the heavier elements are relatively rare. Although the big bang theory is regarded as the best explanation scientists have of the history of the universe, it shouldn't be regarded as beyond dispute. Some scientists do not accept it.

The Bible and the big bang

Does the big bang theory contradict the Bible, or is it consistent with Scripture, at least to some extent?[12]

The most important point of agreement is that both beliefs indicate that the universe had a beginning, that it isn't eternal. On some other points, the two accounts may be taken as complementary. The big bang theory provides no explanation for the origin of the universe, while the Bible identifies God as its Creator. The theory doesn't explain why the universe is so finely designed for life, while the Bible indicates that God intended it to support living organisms.

One important point where there may be conflict between the Bible and the big bang theory is the amount of time involved. Scientists have no explanation for what made the universe begin, but given a starting point, they have calculated that presently observed processes would take about 13.7 billion years to produce the universe as we now observe it. The extent of conflict with Genesis 1:1 depends on how that text is interpreted. However, any proposal that restricts the Creator to the processes described in the big bang theory will unavoidably conflict with the teaching of Scripture that God is absolutely sovereign over creation and its "laws."

The idea that God could have created the universe using a process something like the big bang might be consistent with some interpretations of Genesis 1:1. However, some conflict is unavoidable due to rejection of the supernatural events of Creation week by those who hold the big bang theory. Both the "ecosphere creation" and "solar system creation" interpretations allow for creation of the universe before Genesis 1:1. The "universe creation" interpretation could allow for the earth to exist in a lifeless state for some unknown period of time between Genesis 1:1 and Genesis 1:2. The big bang model might describe what happened during that time gap, but there would still be a conflict over the timing of the events of Creation week. There is probably no way to harmonize the big bang theory with the interpretation that the entire universe was created at the beginning of the six-day Creation of Genesis 1. But, as we noted earlier in this chapter, the "universe creation" doesn't fit some of the biblical data well either. The position favored here is that, regardless of which interpretation of Genesis 1:1 one prefers, the universe wasn't created during Creation week, but at a previous time.

Conclusions

Genesis 1:1 is one of the most profound statements in Scripture. It identifies God as the Creator of all, implying His eternal existence, His omnipotence, and His creative wisdom. It explains the order and design so clearly seen in the universe. It confirms our intuition that there is a reason for our existence and reminds us that our scientific reach is limited. It is the foundation upon which we build our view of reality and our place in the universe.

---

1. This argument was famously made by Thomas Aquinas in *Summa Theologica,* First Part, Question 2, Article 3.

2. For recent thinking, see Grossman, L. "Death of the Eternal Cosmos." *New Scientist* 213 (January 14, 2012):6, 7.

3. E.g., Psalm 33:6–9; John 1:1–13; Colossians 1:16; Hebrews 11:3.

4. Shea, WH. "A Comparison of Narrative Elements in Ancient Mesopotamian Creation-Flood Stories With Genesis 1-9." *Origins* 11(1984):9–29; Copan, P. and WL. Craig. *Creation Out of Nothing.* Grand Rapids, MI: Baker (2004), 29–36.

5. Andreasen, N-E. "The Word 'Earth' in Genesis 1:1." *Origins* 8(1981):13–19; Hasel, GF. "The Meaning of Genesis 1:1." *Ministry* 49/1(1976):21–24; Roth, AA. *Origins: Linking Science and Scripture.* Hagerstown, MD: Review and Herald® (1998), 316; Regalado, FO. "The Creation Account in Genesis 1: Our World Only or the Universe?" *Journal of the Adventist Theological Society* 13/2(2002):108–120.

6. Davidson places the gap between verses 2 and 3; Davidson, RM. "The Biblical Account of Origins," *Journal of the Adventist Theological Society* 14/1(2003):4–43; see also Younker, RW. *God's Creation: Exploring the Genesis Story,* Nampa, ID: Pacific Press® Publishing Association (1999), 33–35.

7. See Copan, P. and WL. Craig (2004).

8. "Ecosphere" refers to all the earth's living organisms and their physical environment.

9. See White, EG. *Patriarchs and Prophets.* Nampa, ID: Pacific Press® (2002), chapters 1–3.

10. Roth, AA. *Science Discovers God.* Hagerstown, MD: Autumn House, (2008); Heeren, F. *Show Me God.* 2nd ed. Wheeling, IL: Daystar Publications (2000).

11. Numerous references can be found on the Internet.

12. See de Groot, M. "The Big Bang Model: An Appraisal." *College and University Dialogue* 10/1(1998):9–12.

CHAPTER 2

The First Three Days

When first created, the earth wasn't suitable for life. It was "un-formed" and "unfilled" (*tohu wa bohu*), dark and covered with water (Genesis 1:2).[1] We aren't told how long the earth remained in this state; some readers see only a few moments, while others see a long period of time. Neither are we told why God didn't speak the earth into existence in a fully formed state, but chose instead to use a period of six days to prepare it and furnish it with life. Perhaps God purposefully worked and rested as an example, a model, for the humans He planned to place in charge of the earth.

The idea of transforming a lifeless planet into one that can support life, a concept called *terraforming,* has been a topic of science fiction for decades. NASA has even been interested in the possibility of preparing Mars for human habitation. The major concerns are providing a suitable atmosphere, warmth, and water. Long before humans ever thought of terraforming, God prepared our earth for life through a series of creative acts.

The first hint of transformation comes when the text mentions that God's Spirit was "moving" or "hovering" (*rachaph*) over the waters. This "hovering" can be compared with the hovering of an eagle over her nest as she cares for her young (see Deuteronomy 32:11). The presence of God's Spirit is an indication that God is ready to act. Creation doesn't occur apart from the presence of God.

Day 1: Let there be light

The first step God took in preparing the earth for life was to provide light. God spoke, and the dark earth was lighted. Paul refers to this event, saying that God "commanded light to shine out of darkness" (2 Corinthians 4:6). There is no hint of a gradual process. God speaks and it is done (Psalm 33:6–9).

We need not suppose that God invented light at this time. Light is one of the attributes of God's presence. Psalm 104:2 describes God as covering Himself with light as a garment. Light must have existed before our world was created because God existed before the creation (see John 1:1–5). Furthermore, the Bible seems to suggest that the events of Creation week occurred after the creation of the universe. God refers to the existence of other beings who saw the creation of our world,[2] and Lucifer had already fallen when Eve met him in the Garden (Genesis 3:1–7; Ezekiel 28:11–14). The fact that the universe already existed implies that light did too. It was the earth, not the universe, that was dark.

The Bible doesn't identify the source of the light, but there are at least two possibilities. The light could have come from God Himself. As noted above, light is associated with God's presence. In the future creation, God's glory so illuminates the New Jerusalem that there's no need for sun or moon (Revelation 21:23). God's presence can produce either light or darkness. For example, during the Exodus, He was a light at night and a cloud during the day (Exodus 13:21). Jesus' statement, "I am the light of the world" (John 8:12), may be more than a metaphor.

Another potential source for the light is the sun. I'll discuss the relationship of light to the sun, along with the events of Creation day 4, in the next chapter.

Whatever the source, God declared that the light was good. The organisms that God planned to create needed to have light. The goodness of the light—its appropriateness for life—can be seen in its properties.

Consider some of the characteristics of light that make it especially suitable as a source of energy for living organisms. First, light contains just the amount of energy appropriate for living organisms. Its energy level is low enough not to damage the molecules that comprise the bodies of living organisms, yet high enough to trigger photosynthesis, which is necessary for life. We can observe our environment without being cooked in the process.

A second characteristic of light that reveals it is designed to support life is its ability to travel through empty space. Most familiar forms of energy, such as sound and mechanical and electrical energy, are transmitted by matter and cannot travel through empty space. But light can, and that makes it possible to have an energy source large enough to supply the entire world but distant enough to dilute that energy to a level that's safe for life.

We don't know whether the light that shone on earth during the first three days of Creation week came from God's presence or from some other source; but now it is the sun that lights the earth, and in the light it produces, we see an evidence of design in creation. Light is a form of electromagnetic radiation. This radiation can be produced in many different energy levels, ranging from low-energy radio waves through visible light to high-energy X-rays and gamma rays. However, most of the sun's energy production is in the visible spectrum, making it a good source of energy for our world. It also produces some infrared radiation, which provides heat for the earth, and some ultraviolet light, which can be dangerous to life but is useful in small amounts. That most of the light that the sun produces is in the visible range and is evidence that it is here by design.

Another evidence that sunlight is designed for life is its relationship to the temperature at which life can exist. The earth's temperature depends on a number of factors, among them its distance from the sun, its rate of rotation, the composition of its atmosphere, and the distribution on it of land and sea. In order for life to exist, the intensity of the output of the sun must be in balance with all the other factors so that the resulting temperature is suitable for life. Because of this combination of factors, the earth has this balance. None of the other planets of our solar system do.[3]

Day 2: Let there be an expanse

God spoke again, and the waters above were separated from those below. This is the creation of the "expanse," best understood as the atmosphere, where water is suspended in the clouds, where the birds fly, and where the sun and moon appear.

The Hebrew word *raqia'* is used to describe the means by which God separated the waters above from the waters below. This word can sometimes have the meaning of something spread out or drawn into a thin sheet. Some critics have claimed that the Hebrews of old viewed the cosmos as a flat surface covered with a solid dome,[4] and these critics say that this view is reflected in the biblical account of Creation. They conclude, then, that because these ancient Hebrews were wrong, we can't trust the biblical account of Creation, so we should reject a literal interpretation of the biblical account.

However, it is the critics' claim that should be rejected.[5] In the first place, the logic is flawed. Whether or not the ancient Hebrews regarded the sky as a solid dome has no bearing on the question of whether God created in six days. Regardless of the details, the waters *were* separated on the second day of Creation week, and the atmosphere still keeps them apart. Second, the premise itself is dubious. Recent scholarship has shown that the Hebrews did *not* believe that the sky was a solid dome with windows; they recognized that clouds are the source of rain.[6] Third, the supposition that the interpretations of the ancient Hebrews exhaust the meaning of the text is pernicious. The Bible itself says that the prophets, including those who wrote the Bible, didn't always fully understand what they were told to communicate (Daniel 12:8; 1 Peter 1:10–12).

The atmosphere provides one of the most crucial requirements for life—a supply of oxygen. It also functions to distribute the oxygen, other gases, and water to all parts of the earth's surface. The water cycle depends on the atmosphere's distribution of water vapor to the entire world.

Our atmosphere shows design in a variety of ways. First, it contains an appropriate proportion of oxygen. As is true of other elements essential for life, the amount of oxygen in our environment is critical. We must have enough to support life, but not so much that it becomes toxic. High levels of oxygen would also make it difficult to extinguish fires. Our planet is the only known planet with oxygen levels anywhere close to what humans and other land animals need.

The amount of nitrogen in our atmosphere—almost 80 percent—is also beneficial for life. Nitrogen is not very reactive, so it is safe for us to breathe. This makes it a good medium through which to distribute the other gases needed by living organisms. Nitrogen is also an important component of proteins and nucleic acids, hence it provides vital nutrition to both plants and animals. Nitrogen-fixing bacteria and lightning strikes chemically convert atmospheric nitrogen into compounds useful to plants. It is doubtful that life could survive very long if the nitrogen were removed from our atmosphere.

Another beneficial feature of our atmosphere is the rarity of toxic gases. Most of earth's atmosphere is made up of gases that, at the levels at which they exist, don't harm life. Some toxic gases enter the atmosphere from volcanoes and decaying organic material, but these gases are quickly neutralized, restoring a healthy atmosphere. Some human activities also produce toxic gases, but this is not the result of God's creation activities. Fortunately, there are natural mechanisms that help purge these toxic gases from the atmosphere when they're no longer being produced.

To be suitable for life, earth must have an atmosphere. The appropriate levels of oxygen and nitrogen in earth's atmosphere, the rarity of toxic gases, and the interaction of the atmosphere with other features of the physical environment all bear witness to divine design.

Day 3: Let the dry land appear

Again God speaks, and the waters are drawn away and the continents rise above the level of the sea. We infer great movements of the earth's crust as ocean basins were formed and filled with water, and the land exposed. And God declares they are good. They are suited to the needs of the diverse living creatures God intends to create.

Design can be seen in both the land and the sea. Earth has enough water to cover the entire planet to a depth of more than two kilometers (more than one mile). Dry land can exist because of differences in the composition of the rocks that form its crust. The continents are made largely of granite, sandstone, and shale, which have a lower density than do the rocks that comprise the sea floor. The latter is made largely of relatively high-density rocks such as basalt. Both kinds of rock "float" upon the semiplastic mantle, the lighter rocks floating higher than the denser rocks, thus producing continents and ocean basins, respectively. We shouldn't regard the presence of dry land on earth as due to chance. The structure of the rocks evidences design, which is also seen in the fact that the elements in the earth's crust are present roughly in proportion to the needs of living organisms.[7]

Water is one of the most familiar examples of design. Among its most remarkable properties is the fact that it can exist as a solid, liquid, or gas at temperatures in the range at which life can survive. Water's high-heat capacity helps prevent wild swings of temperature where it exists in sufficient quantity. Because ice floats, aquatic life can survive in the liquid water beneath the ice floating on lakes and seas. Water's transparency enables light to reach depths of up to three hundred feet (about one hundred meters), expanding the productive zone of the oceans. Ocean water also helps to stabilize levels of carbon dioxide by absorbing and releasing it. And water is an excellent solvent, which means it can transport materials from place to place.

The separation of the sea and the dry land was an important step in making the planet a habitat suitable for living creatures. We can see design in the rocks of the earth and in the remarkable properties of water.

Day 3: Let the earth bring forth vegetation

The Bible says God gave a second command on the third day of Creation week, one that resulted in the creation of vegetation. In the biblical narrative, plants are linked with the soil or ground both in the description of their creation and also in the record of the curses brought on by sin.[8] Despite this close linkage, separate divine commands are given. Life doesn't spontaneously sprout from the ground; it does so only at God's command.[9] There is a huge difference between what's living and what isn't.

Earth's vegetation was diverse from the beginning—herbs bearing seeds and trees bearing fruit. There is no hint that one or a few simple ancestral plants evolved over long ages into the diversity seen today. By the end of that third day, the plants were in place. Three days later, God gave them to the humans and land animals for food. And once more, God was satisfied with His creation and pronounced it good.

Animals cannot survive without plants. Both play important roles in the oxygen cycle. In the chemical process called photosynthesis, plants produce the oxygen animals must have. Animals use this oxygen, producing carbon dioxide from it, which, in turn, the plants take up and convert it back to oxygen. Plants also provide nutrients for animals. They take in nutrients from the soil and air and convert them into products animals need for energy, growth, and maintenance. And plants recycle nutrients from animal wastes and decaying matter, producing from them the nutrients that animals need but cannot produce themselves, thus preventing these "wastes" from accumulating, from going to waste, which would limit the nutrients available to animals.

Plants are also valuable producers of many different kinds of molecules useful to humans, especially in maintaining health and resisting disease. More than a hundred plant-derived drugs are in current use. Such drugs as aspirin, quinine, digitalis, and ephedrine have been important in treating diseases. Many other plant products are also beneficial for our health, including many yet to be identified. Truly, plants are designed to support animal life.

Comments on the text

The language of the Creation narrative seems to be phenomenological[10] —the language of appearance—rather than technical or analytical. Scripture presents the events of the Creation days as real events described in the language of the writer's culture. Some scholars attempt to discredit the Creation story on the basis that it is not scientific, but this is a *non sequitur*. It is the real world that Scripture describes. It is real history, even if the language is nontechnical. We can understand what is meant by inferring what kinds of events would fit the language used to describe them.

"And God said." Throughout the Creation narrative, God acts by fiat—by command. As He speaks, the creation is formed. Through Isaiah, God says that His word will accomplish what He pleases (Isaiah 55:11). There is no conflict in the Bible's story of Creation, whether with other gods or with light or darkness or matter. There is only one God, and the work of creation is completely under His control. There is not even potential for a conflict because all that exists is upheld by His power (Colossians 1:17; Hebrews 1:3).

"And God saw." Seven times during the Creation week, God declared that what He had made was good. The goodness of creation reflects God's satisfaction with it. God looked at what He had created and declared that it suited His purpose, which was to make the world a place to be inhabited (Isaiah 45:18).

"And God called." God gave names to various parts of the physical environment. Giving names is a prerogative of whoever is in charge. God, not a human, named the day, the night, the heavens, the earth, and the sea. In so doing, God indicated that He is the God of time (day and night) and space (the heavens, the earth, and the sea).[11] We may affect them to some extent, but we cannot manipulate them. They are under God's control. It is He who makes the sun to shine and the rain to fall on both the just and the unjust (Matthew 5:45). It is He who can change the position of the sun relative to the earth (Joshua 10:13; 2 Kings 20:11). It is He who owns the land (Psalm 24:1) and sets the boundaries of the sea (Psalm 104:9).

Conclusions

Although our attention is drawn to the events of the Creation week, we shouldn't overlook what creation says about God. He is the Sovereign Creator. At His word, the physical world is transformed as He intends. There is no delay, no conflict, no resistance. He creates deliberately, purposefully, and through an organized sequence of commands. His handiwork is good, without flaw, and fully functional. The events of the first three days of Creation week revealed God's wisdom and power as He transformed the dark, wet world into one that was organized and ready to be inhabited by living creatures. Design is evident in everything He does, including His forming of the physical environment in preparation for life.

1. Cf. Job 38:9; 2 Peter 3:5.

2. Job 38:4–7. Cf. Job 1:6; 2:1, where the "sons of God" are mentioned as meeting in heavenly council, with Satan apparently claiming to represent this world. Also see 1 Corinthians 4:9.

3. We know very little about planets outside our solar system, but they are the objects of intense scrutiny.

4. Bull, B. and F. Guy. *God, Sky & Land*. Roseville, CA: Adventist Forum (2011).

5. Sailhamer, JH. *Genesis Unbound*. Sisters, OR: Multnomah Books (1996), 116; Collins, CJ. *Genesis 1–4: A Linguistic, Literary and Theological Commentary*. Phillipsburg, NJ: P&R Publishing (2006), 264; Younker, RW. "Crucial Questions of Interpretation in Genesis 1." Downloaded February 10, 2012, from biblicalresearch.gc.adventist.org/documents.htm#science.

6. Younker, RW. and RM. Davidson. "The Myth of the Solid Heavenly Dome: Another Look at the Hebrew (*raqia'*)." *Andrews University Seminary Studies* 49/1(2011):125–147. The idea of a heavenly dome on a flat earth can be traced to nineteenth-century authors who were disputing the reliability of the Bible.

7. Denton, MJ. *Nature's Destiny: How the Laws of Biology Reveal Purpose in the Universe*. NY: The Free Press (1998), 78.

8. Genesis 3:17; 4:11, 12. Generally, the Hebrews did not regard plants as alive because they do not have breath or blood.

9. Lennox, JC. *Seven Days That Divide the World*. Grand Rapids, MI: Zondervan (2011), 70.

10. See Collins (2006), 260–265.

11. Turner, L. *Back to the Present*. Grantham, England: Autumn House (2004), 18, 21.

CHAPTER 3

The Second Three Days

Many scholars have seen a pattern in the sequence of creation events. The first three days were devoted to *forming* the world and the second three days to *filling* it.[1] Further, there is a parallelism in the sequence of topics. The first and fourth days refer to light, the second and fifth days deal with the sky and seas, and the third and sixth days focus on the land. This pattern may reflect the wording in Genesis 1:2, where the earth is described as "unformed and unfilled." However, the pattern in the Creation sequence is not a rigid structure that the Creation events were forced to fit, but rather reflects a creative sequence that formed a pattern. That the pattern is not rigid is illustrated by the fact that the sky was formed on day 2 but the sun and moon are mentioned on day 4. Also the seas were formed on day 3 but filled on day 5. Nevertheless, we can see a pattern, and the exceptions to the pattern are evidence that the pattern is real and not contrived.

Day 4: Let there be lights

On the fourth day, God made the sun and moon to be signals to humans and other living organisms. Much debate has centered on the question of whether the sun and moon came into existence on the fourth day, or whether they already existed and were subject to some change on that day. There is no logical contradiction here; several explanations can be proposed. The difficulty is that we don't know which one, if any, is correct. The Hebrew text permits some leeway in interpretation.[2]

One view is that the sun was created prior to day 4,[3] but on the fourth day was appointed to its function of dividing the light and darkness.[4] It may have provided light before day 4, or it may have been dark at first and appeared in its full light when the atmosphere cleared on the fourth day. This explanation can be incorporated into any of the creation models except those that rely on the sun coming into existence on Creation day 4.

The other major view is that the sun was created on day 4. We already noted[5] that God's presence is light, and that the light of His presence may be expressed in a diurnal cycle of light and darkness. There was no need for another light source as long as God was present. Another possibility is that there was a temporary light source that functioned until the sun was created. We may be uncertain about which view is correct, but there is no logical contradiction here.

The stars are mentioned in the description of day 4, but the Hebrew text doesn't indicate whether the stars were created on that day or at some prior time. The text says something like, "God made . . . the lesser light to govern the night, and the stars." This could be interpreted to mean that the moon would govern the night with the stars.[6] The Bible is clear that the stars were created (John 1:1–3; Psalm 148:1–5) and that they are not gods, but are dependent on the Creator God.

The sun and moon are not named in Genesis 1, but merely referred to as the "greater light" and the "lesser light." In the ancient world, the sun and moon bore the names of gods. Because it seems so apparent that the Genesis account deliberately avoids naming the sun and the moon, many scholars believe Moses intentionally worded the account this way to oppose the sun worship of the surrounding cultures.[7] These heavenly bodies are not gods; they're the servants of the Creator God, created to do His bidding, to divide the day and the night, to be markers of time, and to provide signals to the living creatures.

Both the sun and the moon are designed to support life. The contribution that light makes was described in the discussion about the first day.[8] Sunlight can travel a great distance through space, providing energy and carrying signals to the inhabitants of the distant earth. The main energy output of the sun is strong enough to supply life on earth but not so strong as to injure life.

It is less often noted that the moon is also designed for life.[9] The moon functions as a time signal, dividing the year into months. It also produces the ocean tides, which provide signals to regulate the behavior of many organisms. The reproductive behavior of sea turtles, certain fish, certain worms, and many other marine creatures is regulated by changes in the moon's position and its effects on the tides. The tides also help create beaches and move materials onto and away from the beaches, effectively cleaning them.

Although the moon's benefits are not as obvious as those of the sun, it does evidence its being designed to support life on the earth.

Day 5: Creatures of the sea and sky

Creatures of the sea and sky were created on the fifth day. God spoke, and the waters abounded with many kinds of living organisms. He spoke again, and the flying animals came into being. The text speaks of *kinds* (plural) of creatures present from the beginning. There is no support for the notion that only one kind was created in the beginning and all other kinds evolved from it. The original creation was diverse, with a great variety of kinds of life.

Design in living creatures is such a familiar and obvious feature that we need say little about it here. Birds show amazing design for flight. Porpoises have a wonderful sonar system that enables them to find their way in the darkness of the waters. All creatures, great and small, are designed for their role in the overall ecology. Further, even in our fallen world the ecological interactions themselves appear designed to support living creatures.

Day 6: Let the earth bring forth living creatures

On the sixth day, God's creative fiat is heard once more. This time, living creatures are formed from the dust (Genesis 2:19) and given the breath of life.[10] Note that diversity is mentioned from the beginning. There were different kinds of wild beasts and different kinds of cattle and of creeping things. When God created the land creatures, He created them in diversity and abundance, as He had the creatures of the sea and sky.

We marvel at the design seen in all living creatures, including those that live on the dry ground. Although our world is tainted by the effects of sin, we can still see design in the creatures of the land, from the elephant to the monkey, from the bat to the horse, and from the rabbit to the fox. We see design even in the lion and the bear, and wonder what they could be in a world free from sin and violence.[11]

Finally, God created humans in His own image to represent Himself in managing the other creatures. We'll discuss the creation of humans in chapter 5.

The phrase "according to their kinds,"[12] or its equivalent, is applied to the plants, the aquatic creatures, the flying creatures, and the land animals. In context, there were various "kinds" of plants, each of which produced their own kind of fruit or seed. The animals were created in "kinds." Nothing is said about whether the various kinds would change or remain the same. The point is that God created a diversity of living kinds during the third, fifth, and sixth days of Creation.

Many have questioned whether the "kinds" of Genesis are the same as our "species." The answer is No.[13] In the realm of science, a *species* is defined by whether or not it interbreeds with other species. Groups of the same "kind" that are isolated from each other may lose the ability to interbreed and therefore be regarded as different species. The dog family provides a familiar example. The wild dogs of India don't naturally interbreed with those of Japan or South America; each area has its own species. Taxonomic categories such as species, genus, and family are created by biologists and don't have any consistent relationship to the biblical term *kinds*.

God didn't simply leave His creatures to fend for themselves. He provided them with food in the form of green plants. To the humans, He specifically mentioned that food included every plant yielding seed and every tree producing fruit. More generally, green plants were provided for every beast of the earth and every bird of the sky and everything that moves on the land. There is no hint of predation or violence or death. That the life in the world God created was characterized by peace and tranquility is seen in the picture of God speaking the creation into existence, in the relationships among the creatures, and in the provision of plant food for all of them.

Day 7: God rested

On the seventh day, God rested from the work He had been doing. The creation was now completed, and He could take satisfaction in what He had made. It was at this time that He instituted the Sabbath rest.[14] The text says God rested from His work of creating (Genesis 2:2, 3). This doesn't mean that He withdrew from the world. He continued to work in it, guiding His people (Matthew 28:20), sending the rain and the sun (John 5:17), and sustaining the existence of the universe (Colossians 1:16, 17). This text rules out the philosophy of deism, which claims that God created and then left the world to operate on its own. The world has nothing of its own on which to operate. It also rules out the philosophy of evolutionary creation, which claims God continues to create now in the same way He has always worked, using gradual processes to produce new kinds of plants and animals. Contrary to this philosophy, God's actions in sustaining the universe, including living beings, differ from those He used to bring the universe and living beings into existence.[15]

At the end of the sixth day, when everything was in place, the Creator declared that what He had created was very good. There are several features of His creation that we would regard as good. First, God created through peaceful means—through divine fiats. Creation didn't involve violence or struggle. Second, the world God created was well designed to support life, with appropriate amounts of energy, oxygen, living space, diversity, and food. Third, God appointed a responsible and capable manager, Adam, to care for the creatures. Fourth, the "kingdom" God created was peaceful; there was no violence among the creatures. Fifth, to maintain a regular schedule among the living organisms, God set the sun and moon in place to signal the daily, monthly, and yearly cycles.

The goodness of creation can still be seen in part, but the effects of sin have introduced evil into creation, and it can no longer be properly called "very good" as it was originally.[16]

In a sense, all creation was blessed when God declared it "very good," but on three of the days of Creation week, God gave special blessings. First, He blessed the creatures of the sea and sky. This was a blessing of their reproduction and territorial expansion. In the ancient world, fertility was regarded as a great blessing. God's blessing meant that even after the creatures of earth became subject to death, they wouldn't cease to exist but they would instead multiply and populate the earth.

Second, God blessed the humans. This blessing included reproduction and territorial expansion, and, in addition, included dominion over the other creatures.

Third, God blessed the seventh day, granting it a special, sacred status. These blessings indicate God's approval. But more than that, they reveal His expectation that we will show our respect for Him in the way we treat our fellow creatures and the way we treat the holy Sabbath day.

The days of Creation have traditionally been interpreted as being literal days. The Hebrew text says, literally, the "evening" and the "morning." Each successive day begins with a new "evening." Each day consists of an "evening," representing a period of darkness and a "morning," representing a period of light—the same kind of days we experience today.[17]

The Creation days are consecutive, comprising a single week. They are numbered consecutively, which elsewhere in the Bible always refers to literal days. The Sabbath commandment, which God wrote with His own hand (Exodus 20:8–11; 31:12–18), tells us to work six days and observe the seventh day as a literal day of rest in commemoration of God's creative work in six days and rest on the seventh. This implies that the days of Creation were literal days. It seems surprising that some scholars doubt that.

The scholars who challenge the idea that we should consider the days of Creation to be literal days suggest several alternative interpretations, but all of them suffer from conflict with physical evidence or flaws in logic or both.[18] For example, the sequence of Creation events doesn't match the sequence in the fossil record, which rules out the theory that the days represent a succession of long ages. In creation, fruit trees came before any animals, while the fossil record shows that animals were buried before fruit trees. The straightforward interpretation that the days of Creation were literal days that comprised one week in time is the best reading of the text.[19]

We often think of the Creation week as consisting of a series of divine actions in which God created the various parts of our universe from nothing. The Bible is clear that God created the universe from nothing (John 1:1–3; Hebrews 11:3), but the descriptions of His creating don't always imply that He created matter in each case. We previously noted that it seems unlikely that God invented light on the first day of Creation.[20] The separation of dry land and seas didn't necessarily require new matter. The formation of the land animals and humans from the dust of the ground seems to indicate that they were created from matter already in existence. God may have created new matter in some cases while using matter He had previously created in other cases. The text seems to allow for both possibilities. This doesn't mean that God was dependent on uncreated matter. With respect to the Creator God, there is no such thing as matter that "pre-existed" Him. All things were created by Him (John 1:1–3). That means He created all the matter in the entire universe. Therefore He wasn't—He couldn't be— "indebted" to pre-existing matter.[21]

Conclusions

During the fourth through sixth days of that first week, God completed His creation by establishing the sun and moon as signals of time cycles and seasons and by making the many different kinds of living creatures with which He filled the sea, the sky, and the land. Design is apparent in each of the features of creation. The Creation days were literal days, forming a literal week of the same length as the weeks we experience today. The original creation was good in that it functioned according to God's plan; it was complete; and it was free of violence, suffering, and death.[22] God ceased His work of creating on the seventh day and set the Sabbath apart as a continual reminder of what He had done in Creation (Exodus 20:8–11).

1. Noted by many authors; e.g., Davidson, RM. "The Biblical Account of Origins." *Journal of the Adventist Theological Society* 14/1(2003):4–43; Doukhan, JB. "The Genesis Creation Story: Text, Issues, and Truth." *Origins* 55(2004):12–33; Turner, L. *Back to the Present.* Grantham, England: Autumn House (2004), 12–14.

2. Davidson, RM. "Light On the First Day of Creation." *Dialogue* 14/3(2002):24ff.; Collins, CJ. *Genesis 1–4: A Linguistic, Literary, and Theological Commentary.* Phillipsburg, NJ: P&R Publishing (2006), 56–58. See also discussion on "made" and "created" later in this chapter.

3. This could be either on day 1 or as part of an older universe, depending on how Genesis 1:1 is interpreted.

4. Davidson, RM. "Light On the First Day of Creation." *Dialogue* 14/3(2002):24, 33; Doukhan (2004), 27.

5. In chapter 2.

6. See Psalm 136:8, 9; House, CL. "Some Notes on Translating [and the Stars] in Genesis 1:16." *Andrews University Seminary Studies* 25/3(1987):241–248; Davidson, 38; Doukhan (2004), 28.

7. Hasel, GF. "The Polemic Nature of the Genesis Cosmology." *Evangelical Quarterly* 46/2(April–June, 1974):81–102.

8. See chapter 2 of this book.

9. See Comins, NF. *What If the Moon Didn't Exist? Voyages to Earths That Might Have Been.* NY: Harper Perennial (1995).

10. Genesis 7:21, 22 attributes the presence of the breath of life to the birds, land animals, and creeping things.

11. We will look at the problem of predation and natural evil in chapter 7.

12. *min* is the Hebrew word that is translated "kind" in English.

13. Schafer, RD. "The 'Kinds' of Genesis 1: What Is the Meaning of *Min?*" *Journal of the Adventist Theological Society* 14/1(2003):86–100.

14. See chapter 11 of this book.

15. Hebrews 4:3, 4; John 5:17; Copan, P. and WL. Craig. *Creation Out of Nothing.* Grand Rapids, MI: Baker Academic (2004), chapter 4.

16. See chapter 7 of this book.

17. Hasel, GF. "The 'Days' of Creation in Genesis 1: Literal 'Days' or Figurative 'Periods/ Epochs' of Time?" *Origins* 21(1994):5–38; Booth, WM. "Days of Genesis 1: Literal or Non-literal?" *Journal of the Adventist Theological Society* 14(2003):101–120.

18. See Gibson, LJ. "Issues in Intermediate Models of Origins." *Journal of the Adventist Theological Society* 15/1(2005):71–92, for a brief survey; Kidner, D. *Genesis: An Introduction and Commentary.* Downers Grove, IL: InterVarsity Press (1967), 54–58; Collins (2006), 122–129.

19. This is conceded by Walton, JH. *The Lost World of Genesis One.* Downers Grove, IL: InterVarsity Press (2009), 91; and by Sailhammer, JH. *Genesis Unbound.* Sisters, OR: Multnomah Books (1996), 95.

20. See the discussion in chapter 2 of this book.

21. "God was not indebted to pre-existing matter." White, EG. "The Work of Creation," 258, 259, in *Testimonies for the Church,* vol. 8. Mountain View, CA; Pacific Press® (1948).

22. See chapters 6 and 7 of this book for further discussion of death.

CHAPTER 4

Creation Throughout the Bible

Genesis 1–3 is the foundation for the biblical message of salvation, and the echoes from these chapters form a central theme throughout all of Scripture. We will briefly survey some of the biblical texts that refer back to Creation week.[1]

Creation is an important theme in the writings of Moses, even aside from Genesis 1–3. That humans bear God's image is mentioned three times in Genesis.[2] The blessings and curses of Genesis 1–3 are also echoed in other parts of the Pentateuch. The blessing of fertility, in the form of the command to "be fruitful and multiply," was given first to the creatures of sea and sky, and then to Adam and Eve. This blessing was repeated to Noah and his sons as they left the ark (Genesis 9:1), and similar blessings were given to Abraham, Isaac, and Jacob.[3] We see the curse on the ground again when Cain killed his brother (Genesis 4:11, 12), and it is echoed in the name given to Noah.[4]

The Ten Commandments contain a dramatic allusion to Creation week. The reason for "keeping" the seventh-day Sabbath is based on God's work in creating. As He created in six days and rested on the seventh, so humans are to work on six days and rest on the seventh (Exodus 20:8–11). God Himself attested to the Creation week when He spoke the fourth commandment (along with the other nine) from Mount Sinai and then twice wrote it in stone with His own finger (Exodus 31:12–18; 34:28).

When Moses repeated the Ten Commandments in his farewell address, he gave another reason for Sabbath observance—he tied it to God's freeing the Israelites from bondage in Egypt rather than to His work of creation (Deuteronomy 5:12–15; but note that Exodus 20:1, 2 also bases God's call for His people to keep all the law on His freeing them from slavery in Egypt). Creation and Redemption are linked together not only here, but in other biblical contexts as well.[5]

Creation in the Old Testament

The force of opinion in the scientific community has convinced many scholars that the Genesis Creation record is unreliable. Liberal Bible scholars have searched the Bible thoroughly, looking for evidence that it contains creation stories that contradict each other. Probably the most important criticism this search has produced is the claim that Genesis 1 and 2 contradict each other. However, there are good reasons to regard them as complementary rather than contradictory. Let's take a look.

Some critics claim that the sequence of events in Genesis 2 contradicts the sequence of events in Genesis 1. A casual reader might think that Genesis 2 places the creation of Adam before that of the plants and animals, and the creation of Eve after that of everything else (Genesis 2:5–22). This claim reflects a superficial reading. The author of these two chapters isn't likely to have written material he believed to be contradictory. Rather than looking for ways to interpret these passages as contradictory, we ought to begin with the assumption that the author knew what he was doing and cooperate with him[6] by leaning toward interpretations that harmonize with each other.

From this perspective, we see that Genesis 1 refers to the entire Creation week and has obvious chronological markers throughout, while Genesis 2 focuses on the story of the creation of Adam and Eve, introducing other elements of the Creation story only as they were needed. In other words, when Moses wrote Genesis 2, he had other points in mind than the chronological sequence of Creation. Furthermore, in speaking of the plants that were "not yet" in Genesis 2, Moses used terms that indicate he was referring to the weeds and cultivated plants that were developed after Adam's fall.[7] These were plants that had suffered from the curses on the ground and thus were "not yet" in existence at the time of the creation of Adam and Eve on the sixth day of creation. There is no disagreement here, so the claim that Genesis 1 and 2 contradict each other is not sustained.

Creation is an important theme in Job, Psalms, and Proverbs. In Job 38, God questions Job about his knowledge of creation. In verses 4–11, God describes the separation of the land and the sea, an echo of the third day of creation; in verses 12 and 19, He refers to the darkness and the light, which He established on the first day of creation; in Job 39, He describes some of the creatures He made—the mountain goats, the wild donkeys, wild oxen, ostriches, horses, and hawks; in chapter 40, He describes the "behemoth" (probably the hippopotamus),[8] which, He says, "I made along with you"; and in chapter 41, He describes the "leviathan" (probably the crocodile).[9]

The psalms refer to Creation frequently, praising the Creator for His wonderful works, with Genesis 1 as the larger context. They don't tell the story of Creation—they assume it. Psalm 104 is the most extensive psalm of praise to the Creator,[10] but many other psalms contain echoes of Genesis 1. They identify the Lord who "made heaven and earth" (Psalm 121:1). The psalms tell *how* God created, saying He created by fiat—He spoke and it was done (Psalms 33:6–9; cf. 148:5). They say that God created the day and the night (Psalm 74:16; 104:20), as described in the record of what occurred on the first day. God "lays the beams of His upper chambers[11] in the waters" and "makes the clouds His chariot" (Psalm 104:3)[12]—a poetic reference to Creation day 2. God divided the land and sea (Psalms 95:5; 104:5–9)—the third day of creation. He made the sun and also summer and winter (Psalm 74:16, 17), and He appointed the moon and the stars and ordained them to rule the night (Psalms 8:3; cf. 104:19; 136:7–9), a reminder of Creation day 4. God gave humans dominion over the other creatures (Psalm 8:6), an echo from the sixth day of creation. And a psalmist reminds us of the linkage of Creation and the Sabbath by quoting the wording of Exodus 20:11: "Who made heaven and earth, the sea, and all that is in them" (Psalm 146:6).

Isaiah speaks of the God who "created the heavens and stretched them out, who spread forth the earth and that which comes from it" (Isaiah 42:5). God makes light and darkness (Isaiah 45:7). He says, "I have made the earth, and created man on it. It was I—My hands that stretched out the heavens, and all their host I have commanded" (Isaiah 45:12). God "did not create it [the earth] in vain" but "formed it to be inhabited" (Isaiah 45:18). Creation is also important to Isaiah's vision of the future, when "the wolf also shall dwell with the lamb" (Isaiah 11:6) and God will create "new heavens and a new earth" (Isaiah 65:17).

The writings of other prophets refer to Creation as well. Jeremiah speaks of God's power and wisdom in making the earth and stretching out the heavens (Jeremiah 51:15). Amos refers to God as Creator of the Pleiades and Orion (Amos 5:8) and the One who "builds His layers in the sky" (Amos 9:6). Jonah identified himself as one who worships the God of heaven, "who made the sea and the dry land" (Jonah 1:9). Zechariah points to the Lord as the One "who stretches out the heavens" and "lays the foundation of the earth" (Zechariah 12:1). And Nehemiah makes a clear allusion to the Sabbath commandment of Exodus 20: "You have made heaven, . . . the earth and all things on it, the seas and all that is in them" (Nehemiah 9:6). Thus Creation is woven throughout the Old Testament.

Creation in the New Testament

Jesus clearly affirmed the Genesis Creation account. He referred to the creation of humans: "He who made them at the beginning made them male and female" (Matthew 19:4–6; Mark 10:6–9). Jesus quoted from Genesis 1:27 and 2:24, thus showing the two chapters are complementary. He also stated "the Sabbath was made for man, not man for the Sabbath" (Mark 2:27, 28). The example of Jesus Himself is sufficient affirmation of the truthfulness of the Genesis Creation story.

Luke referred to Adam, the first human, as "the son of God" (Luke 3:38). And in his book of Acts, he pictures Peter and John appealing to God as Creator when threatened with persecution: "Lord, You are God, who made heaven and earth and the sea, and all that is in them" (Acts 4:24). This is another allusion to the Sabbath commandment in Exodus

20. Paul and Barnabas used the same theme when the people of Lystra wished to worship them (Acts 14:15). And Paul appealed to the Creator God in his sermon to the Stoics and Epicureans on Mars' Hill (Acts 17:24–31). It is significant that Jesus and His closest followers believed in and affirmed the story of Creation as given in Genesis.

John started his Gospel with an echo of Genesis 1:1—"In the beginning . . ." The Creator, the One who "became flesh and dwelt among us," was the Word (John 1:1–3, 14). John emphasized the creative power of Jesus in the stories he chose for his Gospel. Creation is seen in His turning the water to wine, in the new birth, in the offer of living water, in the healings, in the feeding of the five thousand, in the walking on the sea, and in the raising of Lazarus.[13] Each of these examples was effected by the Word, literally through His words of command—which is reminiscent of the creation by fiat pictured in Genesis 1.

Paul referred several times to the story of Creation and the Fall. He identified Adam as the first man (1 Corinthians 15:45) and says he was formed before Eve (1 Timothy 2:3). He quoted the statement in Genesis 2:24 that husband and wife shall be "one flesh" (Ephesians 5:31). He said that sin and death entered the world through Adam's sin (Romans 5:12; 1 Corinthians 15:22), with the result that the entire creation is now groaning under the curse (Romans 8:20–22). Paul also referred to the time when God "commanded light to shine out of darkness" (2 Corinthians 4:6). His affirmation of the Creation story is particularly important in helping us to understand the problem of natural evil—the "groaning" of creation.[14]

The writer of Hebrews[15] affirmed the Creation story as given in Genesis. He referred to "the beginning," when God "laid the foundation of the earth" (Hebrews 1:10),[16] and made one of the clearest statements in Scripture of creation *ex nihilo* (from nothing): "By faith we understand that the worlds were framed by the word of God, so that the things which are seen were not made of things which are visible" (Hebrews 11:3). He also referred to the dominion given to man at Creation, "you . . . set him over the works of Your hands" (Hebrews 2:6–8).[17] And in a discussion of the Sabbath, he refers to God's rest on the seventh day (Hebrews 4:3, 4). This is an important reference to Genesis 2:1–3, because it indicates that God's work during Creation week differed from His work of sustaining the world.[18]

James referred to the creation of humans in the image of God (James 3:9). And Peter wrote a strong statement about skepticism in the last days, predicting that people would deny that God acts in history—they won't believe in the Second Advent because they don't believe in Creation and the Flood, but "willfully forget: that by the word of God the heavens were of old, and the earth standing out of water [Creation] and in the water [the Flood]" (2 Peter 3:5). Nevertheless, Peter looked for the creation of "new heavens and a new earth" (verse 13).

Revelation refers both to the old creation and to the new creation. John repeated the language of Exodus 20, writing of the One "who created heaven and the things that are in it, the earth and the things that are in it, and the sea and the things that are in it" (Revelation 10:6). The messages of the three angels comprise the focal point of the book (Revelation 14:6–12).[19] The first message, "worship Him who made heaven and earth, the sea . . ." is a clear allusion to the Sabbath commandment in Exodus 20, linking the Sabbath with Creation. The book concludes with a description of the new creation, where again there is no death or suffering and God is present with His people (Revelation 21; 22).

The Bible starts with Creation (Genesis 1–3) and ends with Creation (Revelation 21; 22). This act of God isn't confined to a discreet portion of Scripture in isolation from the rest of God's Word; instead, it is foundational to all that Scripture says. Imagine how difficult it would be to explain the meaning of all the allusions to and echoes of Genesis 1–3 if we lacked those chapters. Creation is not a peripheral idea in Scripture, but is central to both worship and salvation—which are key themes of the book.

Creation and science

Creation, by definition, is a supernaturally caused event. Science, by current definition, is naturalistic. One should expect tension between ideas that are based on such profoundly different presuppositions. Happily, most scientific questions are experimental in nature and don't produce conflict between Creation and scientific naturalism. Tension between these two belief systems is restricted to historical questions, such as explaining the origin of a particular physical feature and estimating when an event occurred.

Conflict arises when presuppositions that differ yield conflicting interpretations. For example, every living organism has genetic information that specifies the form and function of that organism. Curiously, the genetic code (the mechanism used to translate the genetic information) is nearly identical in all living organisms. Creationists consider this to be the case because the code is intelligently designed and appropriate for all forms of life. Naturalistic scientists, on the other hand, say that this is so because all organisms have evolved from an ancestor they all have in common.

Conflict also arises when observations seem inconsistent with Scripture. For example, radioisotope dating of rocks often points to ages in the hundreds of millions of years. Creationists don't have a fully satisfactory explanation for radioisotope dates, but other evidence points to earth's existing for a much shorter time.[20]

There are also other challenges to the creationist theory for which we don't yet have satisfactory answers. Creationists have responded in a variety of ways. The response I favor is to recognize that, by definition, supernatural creation lies outside the boundaries of naturalistic science. God has methods of action that are not accessible to us through either revelation or scientific discovery. Scripture contains what God has told us of His actions in history. Science may help us understand how God governs the world at present, and it may provide hints about the past, but it should be interpreted in the light of Scripture.

When we encounter tension, we should act responsibly.[21] First, claims that conflict with Scripture should be examined thoroughly. Some of these claims are mistaken. Second, we should examine Scripture carefully to see what it actually says about the point in question and to determine the implications of the various views. Third, we should recognize tension where it exists. We don't know everything, and sometimes we have to exercise faith while we wait for more information.

To adopt a view because of our faith in Scripture is consistent with Christian teaching. But to deny tension where it actually does exist is to be irresponsible. Although we can't answer every question, we can expect that continued study will move us toward an understanding of Creation that harmonizes with Scripture.

Conclusion

Creation is the context in which the Bible message is given. It's the first topic of Genesis and the last topic of Revelation. The Bible writers assume the accuracy of the Creation story in Genesis 1 and 2 and often build their teachings on it without repeating or discussing the details. The main points of the Creation story are repeated several times and call for a response from those created in God's image. There is no hint that Genesis 1 is not meant to be taken literally. Those who deny its literal nature are left with the problem of explaining the many other parts of Scripture that refer to it as a literal history. In a real sense, Genesis 1–3 is like a golden cord that binds the biblical story together into a coherent whole. The Creation story recorded in those chapters provides the answers to our deepest questions and is the basis of our deepest hopes.

---

1. See also Shea, WH. "Creation," in *Handbook of Seventh-day Adventist Theology*. GW. Reed, general editor, Hagerstown, MD: Review and Herald® (2000), 418–456.

2. Genesis 1:26, 27; 5:1, 2; 9:6.

3. Genesis 12:1–3; 26:4; and 35:11, respectively.

4. Genesis 5:29. Noah's name means "rest," and his family longed for rest from the toil of working the ground.

5. For example, Psalm 146:6, 7; John 1:1–14; Revelation 14:6, 7.

6. Collins, JC. *Genesis 1–4: A Linguistic, Literary and Theological Commentary*. Phillipsburg, NJ: P&R Publishing (2004), 7.

7. Younker, R. "Genesis 2: A Second Creation Account?" in Baldwin, JT. *Creation, Catastrophe and Calvary: Why a Global Flood Is Vital*. Hagerstown, MD: Review and Herald® (2000), 69–78; Moskala, J. "A Fresh Look at Two Genesis Creation Accounts: Contradictions?" *Andrews University Seminary Studies* 49/1(2011):45–65.

8. Not identified with certainty, but often considered to be the hippo, which is now extinct in Israel.

9. Uncertain identification, but suggestive of the crocodile, which lived in Israel until the early 1900s.

10. Davidson, R. "Creation in Psalm 104," unpublished manuscript presented to the Faith and Science Council, revised October 2010, and currently being prepared for publication in the Biblical Research Institute's book on Creation in the Old Testament, which was expected to be released in 2012.

11. The reference seems to be to God's dwelling above the waters of the sky.

12. Proverbs 8:27–29 also refers to the events of Creation days 2 and 3.

13. Respectively, John 2:6–11; 2:19; 3:3; 4:10; 4:50; 5:1–9; 9:1–7; 6:1–14; 6:15–21; 6:35, 51; and John 11.

14. This problem is virtually intractable for evolutionary theory. See Southgate, C. *The Groaning of Creation: God, Evolution and the Problem of Evil.* Louisville, KY: Westminster John Knox Press (2008).

15. Opinion is divided over whether this was Paul or someone close to him.

16. Quoting Psalm 102:25–27.

17. Quoting Psalm 8:4–6.

18. John 5:17; see also Colossians 1:16, 17; Hebrews 1:3.

19. Paulien, J. *Seven Keys: Unlocking the Secrets of Revelation.* Nampa, ID: Pacific Press® (2009), 111; see also Baldwin, JT. "Revelation 14:7: An Angel's Worldview," in Baldwin (2000), 19–39.

20. Roth, AA. *Origins: Linking Science and Scripture.* Hagerstown, MD: Review and Herald® (1998), chapters 12–15.

21. See Brand, L. *Faith, Reason, and Earth History,* 2nd ed. Berrien Springs, MI: Andrews University Press, 2009.

CHAPTER 5

The Moral Man

Humans are unique. While animals often surprise us by what they can do, only humans have complex language, can think abstractly, and have free will. However, the most important difference between humans and animals may be that only humans worship the Creator. People have suggested various reasons—ranging from chance to divine purpose—for the uniqueness humans have. This is an important issue because the way we view ourselves affects the way we behave, and this affects our well-being, both individually and as societies.

The biblical view of human nature differs radically from views based on the naturalism of evolutionary theory and pantheistic religions. The story of the creation of Adam and Eve in Genesis 1 and 2 is full of purpose, and this gives our lives a richness of meaning not inherent in other views. It gives to us information crucial to understanding our place in the universe.

The story of Creation tells us that God made humans intentionally.[1] We don't exist because of luck or accident. The way God created human beings reveals the value He considers them to have: He created Adam and Eve personally and individually, first Adam and then Eve—forming Adam from the dust of the ground, and then "building" Eve from one of Adam's ribs (Genesis 2:7, 21, 22). Individual personality is an important aspect of human nature.

God formed human beings in His own image, which is another indicator of His regard for humans. Then He gave them "dominion" over the other creatures, entrusting them to their care. All these aspects of the narrative are indicators of God's special regard for the humans He created.[2]

Humans do share some similarities with the animals. Both are described as "living beings" (*nephesh hayyah;* Genesis 1:24; 2:7), made out of the ground (Genesis 2:7, 19), and having the "breath of life" (Genesis 6:17; 7:22). Both have blood, which represents life (Genesis 9:4, 5). But there is a huge distinction between humans and animals in that only humans were made in God's image.

In the image of God created He them

The Members of the Godhead determined to make man "in Our image,"[3] and "according to Our likeness."[4] Despite the huge differences between the Creator and the created, humans are, in some sense, like God. Many people have wondered what this means, and many suggestions have been made.[5]

To be made in the image of God is to be made in relationship. God "made them male and female." Humans are social beings, made for relationships. We form families, social groups, and societies. Perhaps this sociality reflects in some way the relationship among the Trinity. The relational richness of the Godhead is best displayed in a social relationship, not in a group of individualistic beings.[6]

Humans also bear the image of God in the dominion God has granted them over the other creatures (Genesis 1:28).[7] God is the Sovereign King of the universe, with all things under His control, yet He trusted humans with a delegated authority over the other creatures. Humans are God's representatives on this earth. This "dominion" or "stewardship" gives humans an attribute similar to that of God and is rightfully understood as being an aspect of the image of God.

Another aspect of the image of God that humans have is creativity. God is the original Creator, and we see in His handiwork a rich display of beauty in form and color. This creative ability and love of the beautiful is reflected, however faintly, in works of human art and creativity.

Surely, this expression is part of the image of God.

We may also consider humankind's fulfilling the command to "be fruitful and multiply and fill the earth" to be another aspect of creativity. God the Creator gave to His creatures the ability to bring new individual persons into being. God did command the creatures of sea, sky, and land to multiply also, but they don't have the ability to bring new persons into existence. They can produce only more animals, not beings fashioned in God's own image.

Moral judgment is another component of the image of God that humans have as well. Moral judgment entails free will. God gave humans the ability to make decisions for good or for evil, and He taught them the difference. (I'll discuss morality in greater depth later in this chapter.)

Work and rest comprise another aspect of God's image that humans reflect. God works in His world, and He gave humans the responsibility to work also (Genesis 2:15). In addition, as God rested from His work on the seventh day, so humans are to rest from their work on the seventh-day Sabbath. When humans follow the pattern of working six days of the week and resting on the seventh day, they're reflecting the image of God.[8]

Finally, as an image resembles the original in its form, so the human form must share some similarities with that of the Creator. I don't mean to imply that God has five fingers and five toes, but that someone who knows both God and humans would be able to identify similarities in their appearance.

What does the way God created Adam tell us? God created Adam in two steps. First, He formed him from the dust of the earth, and then He breathed into his nostrils the breath of life (Genesis 2:7). Adam wasn't alive until God breathed into him the "life breath." It was then that Adam became a living soul, or a living being. The creation of Adam was not a conversion of some other life form into a human. It was a transformation of nonliving material into a living being.

Scripture doesn't teach that humans are composed of two distinct entities—an animal body and a conscious "soul." The ancient Greeks developed this concept, which, unfortunately, many Christians have added to their belief system.[9] Adam became a "living soul" or a "living being" when God gave him breath.[10] When Adam sinned, God said he would die and return to dust and that his "breath,"[11] or life, would then return to God. Humans don't *have* souls, they *are* souls. The death of a person is the death of a soul.

The unified or holistic nature of humans is further seen in the promise of the resurrection (John 5:28, 29). Jesus' own words indicate the dead are "in the graves." They come forth from their graves to receive their reward. The dead are raised with new spiritual bodies (1 Corinthians 15:42–49) and will be caught up to meet the Lord (1 Thessalonians 4:16, 17). Resurrection doesn't mean the reuniting of a conscious soul with an earthly body that has no consciousness. There is no conscious soul separate from the material body. Resurrection is the re-creation of the whole person, both the physical and the spiritual dimensions of that person. Those dimensions are inseparable.

Creation and the unity of humankind

Humans are diverse. We differ physically, and, more important, in language and culture. Given these differences, we tend to compare ourselves with others and to classify others as superior or inferior. This is all artificial. In reality, we are all descendants of the same parents, Adam and Eve. Adam gave Eve her name, which means "life-giving," because she is the mother of all humans (Genesis 3:20).

Many people wonder whether the differences seen among modern humans could have arisen in the short time between our time and Creation. At one time, biologists did think that humans and other species change very slowly. More recently, it has been discovered that a species can change very rapidly—in the course of a few generations.[12]

Several factors affect the rate of change. One factor is the degree of isolation. In humans, isolation may be geographic—due to distance—or it may be behavioral—due to language or cultural differences. Not so long ago, most humans stayed close to where they were born and married within their cultural group. This practice tends toward inbreeding and naturally results in divergence between isolated populations, whether of humans or any other species. Over time, differences accumulate and eventually produce distinct varieties or races. Humans are subject to these processes as long as they remain in groups that are isolated from each other by distance or language. Thus, while we don't have a historical record of the development of human races, we now know that such changes do not require long ages to develop. In fact, the differences among humans are superficial compared with those of other species. Some 93 percent of our genetic makeup is found in all races; the differences that distinguish the races are minor and involve only about 7 percent of our genes.[13]

The unity of humankind provides a logical basis for the recognition of all humans as bearing the image of God. We are truly all "one blood" (Acts 17:26). There is no basis for any group of humans to believe themselves superior to any other group. In the distant past, Jewish men are said to have thanked God that they were not Gentiles, slaves, or women. The apostle Paul implicitly criticized this prayer, pointing out that no one has special favor with God (Galatians 3:28). Salvation is available on the same terms to both Jews and Greeks, slaves and free, men and women. Jesus' parable of the good Samaritan (Luke 10:25–37) makes the same point: all human beings are worthy of respect and kindness.

Creation and morality

Creation provides the basis for morality. As created beings, we are responsible to our Creator. He has provided the rules of moral behavior. He gave Adam dominion over the other creatures with the instruction to "subdue" (*kabash*), or rule, the earth. God also appointed Adam to till[14] and keep[15] the Garden. This implies responsibility and accountability, which, combined with the gift of free will, are prerequisites for morality.

Morality begins with our responsibility to God the Creator. As creatures, we owe our existence to the Creator. We were created for a purpose—to glorify God (Isaiah 43:7). Our responsibility to God includes the care and management of the created world. God is good, and He created a good world. But due to our moral failure, sin has corrupted this good world. We are called to reduce and, as much as possible, to reverse the evil effects of sin and to nurture the goodness of creation and oppose the evil. In doing this, we witness to the goodness of the Creator.

Our moral accountability also extends to the way we treat other humans, as illustrated in the story of Cain and Abel (Genesis 4:2–12). The image of God is present in all humans, even though it has been defaced by sin. This means that the way we treat others reveals how we feel about God. Because we all have the same first parents and we all are endowed with the image of God, we ought to respect one another and treat one another as members of the same family. God instructs us to demonstrate His love to others through acts of kindness, especially to the weak—the orphans, widows, and disadvantaged (Deuteronomy 15:7–18).[16] In so doing, we allow God to restore His image in us.

Another aspect of creation and morality is our assignment to be fruitful and multiply (Genesis 1:28).[17] The family is intended to serve as a means of maintaining the image of God in the individuals born into this world. Children who grow up in a faithful, God-fearing family will be trained in the development of His image and have the opportunity to fulfill His purpose of bringing glory to Him. Families that fail to train their children properly are responsible for the distortion of God's image that brings dishonor to Him.

Many thinkers have tried to find a basis for a system of morality without reference to God. Aristotle advocated the principles that contribute to a happy, fulfilled life.[18] David Hume proposed that morality could be based on instinct—that we somehow instinctively prefer moral behavior over immoral behavior.[19] Immanuel Kant thought we could determine moral principles through reason and fulfillment of duty.[20] Others have suggested that moral behavior is comprised of the behaviors that result in the greatest good for the most people.

These suggestions have met with varying acceptance, but none of them has been truly successful as a basis for morality, for at least three reasons. First, morality is based on an obligation to some standard, but without a Creator God, there is no enduring standard. Any system of morality based on reason or preference or happiness will be unstable: what was once moral may become immoral, and vice versa, and what contributes to one person's happiness may detract from the happiness of another.

Second, godless moral systems fail because they don't take into account the fallen nature of humans. Human happiness, reason, and preferences don't provide reliable bases for morality because humans are selfish. No system of morality that is flavored with selfishness can be stable.

Third, these systems fail because they subject the minority to the "tyranny of the majority." No moral system can endure long when a significant minority feels oppressed by the dominant majority. The only objective basis for a lasting moral code is the obligation one has to the Creator.

Morality and the Creator

Many people have proposed the idea that evolution rather than Creation provides the true story of origins, but that evolution was successful because God guided the process; it didn't happen by chance. Theories of origins that include this basic idea are widely known as "evolutionary creation" or "theistic evolution." Some theories of evolutionary creation propose that God created gradually, over long ages of time, by guiding the way in which organisms reproduce, struggle for existence, and die. These theories don't consider death to be the result of sin; rather, it is the means the Creator has chosen to bring into existence the creatures He wills. They suggest that death and suffering have always been part of nature and that human behavior has no relationship to natural evil.

However, any theory that makes God the architect of evolution is incompatible with the life and teachings of Jesus as well as with the biblical account of Creation. In the first place, such a theory implies that God has an evil character. The evolutionary process—which is based on violence, suffering, and death—is widely recognized to be evil,[21] so to accuse God of guiding evolution is to accuse Him of being evil.

Second, such theories imply that God wasn't able to create what He wanted directly, but was forced to do it in gradual steps. This makes Him a weakling who can't be depended on to help in response to prayer or to resurrect the dead.

Third, evolutionary creation implies that God holds us to a higher moral standard than He Himself practices. The god of evolutionary theory uses the strong to eliminate the weak, while the God of the Bible expects humans to nurture the weak and condemns them for oppressing the disadvantaged. The god of evolution is immoral by the standard of morality demonstrated by the life and teaching of Jesus, and no one would be satisfied with a moral code based on the character of such a god.

In summary, the god of evolutionary theory doesn't have the qualities of the God of the Bible—omnipotence, omniscience, goodness, and love. In contrast, Jesus showed these qualities, including the power to control nature, such as is evidenced by His stilling the storm on Galilee (Mark 4:35–40) and multiplying the five loaves and two fishes (Matthew 14:13–21). Jesus manifested a high moral character and identified evil as the product of the evil one.[22] The theory that God used evolutionary processes to create must be rejected on moral grounds among other reasons because the evil, death-driven mechanism of evolution is incompatible with the unselfish, life-giving God of the Bible.

Conclusion

Adam and Eve were created individually, on the sixth day of Creation week. They were endowed with features reflecting in a limited way some of the traits of the Creator. They were given dominion over the other creatures, a sacred relationship with each other, a special time for communion with the Creator, and the task of managing the Garden.

Humans are holistic beings, their souls consisting of the combination of the God-given breath of life and the material body. All humans are descendants of Adam and Eve, all carry the image of God, and all are worthy of respect and kindness.

God created us with free will and gave us responsibility, which means we are moral beings and accountable to our Creator for the way we respond to Him, the way we treat each other, and the way we treat the rest of creation. The life and teachings of Jesus Christ, together with the teachings of the divinely inspired prophets, provide the only basis for a stable and satisfying moral code.

1. This is implicit in the statement, "Let Us make man . . ." (Genesis 1:26).

2. Jesus affirmed this in Matthew 10:29–31; Luke 12:6, 7.

3. Hebrew *tselem,* "image," referring to outward resemblance (Genesis 1:26).

4. Hebrew *demuth,* "likeness," referring to inward resemblance (RM. Davidson, personal communication, 2012).

5. E.g., Clines, DJA. "The Image of God in Man," *Tyndale Bulletin* 19(1968):53–103; Feinberg, CL, "The Image of God," *Bibliotheca Sacra* 129(1972): 235–245; Moreland, JP. *The Recalcitrant Imago Dei.* London: SCM Press (2009).

6. See chapter 9 of this book for further discussion of marriage.

7. See chapter 10 of this book.

8. See chapter 11 of this book.

9. Augustine, *City of God;* Aquinas, *Summa Theologica;* downloaded from the Web, December 1, 2011.

10. Hebrew *neishemah,* "breath." In Genesis 6:17 and some other texts, the Hebrew word *ruach* ("wind") is used.

11. Hebrew *ruach,* "wind," "breath," or "spirit." It is present in both humans and animals (Genesis 7:15, 22).

12. See, e.g., Hendry, AP. and MT. Kinnison, "Perspective: The Pace of Modern Life: Measuring Rates of Contemporary Microevolution," *Evolution* 53(1999):1637–1653.

13. See Cavalli-Sforza, LL. *Genes, Peoples, and Languages.* NY: North Point Press (2000); cited in Ridley, M. *Evolution.* Malden, MA: Blackwell Science, Ltd. (2004), 365.

14. Hebrew *'abad,* "to serve, till."

15. Hebrew *shamar,* "to keep," "observe," "take heed," as in "keep the covenant" (Genesis 17:9).

16. Cf. Micah 6:8; Leviticus 19:18.

17. On creation and marriage, see also chapter 9 of this book.

18. See *Ethics* by Aristotle.

19. Hume, David. *An Enquiry Concerning the Principles of Morals* (1751).

20. Kant, Immanuel. *Metaphysics of Morals* (1797).

21. See Huxley, TH. *Evolution and Ethics* (1893).

22. Matthew 13:24–30; 13:36–43; 17:18–21; Mark 1:23–27; Luke 8:26–39; Luke 13:16; John 8:44.

CHAPTER 6

The Loss of Innocence

It seems ironic that so many people deny the existence of a personal devil, while at the same time, interest in the occult and satanic worship seem to be increasing dramatically. The Bible reveals that the devil is real, intelligent, and fully devoted to opposing God's plans to save those who trust in Him.

Satan's efforts to conceal himself began in the Garden of Eden and continue to the present day. At some time in the not-too-distant future, he will be unmasked, and many will say in surprise, "Is this the man who made the earth tremble?" (Isaiah 14:16). At some time in the future, Satan will be destroyed, and the universe will be clean (Isaiah 28:18, 19). But the shortness of the time remaining to him makes him all the more desperate, and in dealing with his wiles we need to be wise (1 Peter 5:8, 9; 2 Corinthians 11:14, 15). To that end, it is instructive to review how he lured our first parents to their ruin.

Genesis 3 opens with a statement about the serpent (*nachash*) being more crafty (*'arum*) than any of the other beasts of the field. This is a curious statement if taken as referring to ordinary reptiles: snakes do not seem to be especially intelligent. The puzzle is cleared up in other parts of Scripture, where Satan is clearly identified as being the serpent (Revelation 20:2).[1] Thus the serpent represents Satan, and there's no doubt that Satan is "more crafty" than any of the animals. The next verses of Genesis 3 show how crafty he was in catching Eve completely off guard.

Has God really said?

The serpent asked Eve a simple question: "Did God really tell you not to eat the fruit of the trees in the Garden?" Questioning whether God has really spoken has led many to ruin. It can be a legitimate question—Jesus strongly warned us about false prophets and false christs (Matthew 24:5, 11, 23–26), and it is important to know what God hasn't said as well as what He has said. However, both the devil and Eve knew what God had said, so Satan's question wasn't sincere. Instead, it was designed to draw Eve into a conversation and give Satan an opportunity to distract her and convince her that though God had spoken, He hadn't spoken truth. Eve's first mistake was in conversing with someone who wanted to lead her to doubt God's word.

Similar questions are asked today in order to raise doubts about the reliability of God's Word. When people wish to insinuate doubts about the truths of the Bible, they often ask questions to the effect of this: "Has God really spoken?" "Is the Bible truly God's Word, or is it merely a collection of Hebrew devotional literature, valued and preserved by the community, but of human origin?" We would be wise to avoid Eve's mistake of being drawn into debates over the reliability of God's Word.

Notice that Satan crafted his question in such a way that Eve would naturally want to respond to it, to correct it. He asked, "Did God tell you not to eat the fruit of any tree of the Garden?" Eve readily replied that, No, God hadn't withheld the fruit of all the trees. Only one tree was forbidden. But the insinuation was that God had established unnecessary rules. The serpent implied that God wanted to keep Eve in servitude lest she become like Him (Genesis 3:5).

Note that this is the very temptation that caused the fall of Satan himself—he wanted to "be like the Most High" (Isaiah 14:14; see also verses 12, 13). Ironically, Eve was already like God in that she was created in His image. God had generously endowed her with some of His own attributes, making her resemble Him in important ways. Yet she came to the conclusion that she could become more like Him through her own efforts.

This is another point on which many of us stumble. We think we can, through our own efforts, improve on what God has given us. A little thought should be sufficient to remind us that we are dependent on God for everything. Just as we have no power to bring ourselves into existence or to take upon ourselves the image of God, so we have no power to make ourselves more like God than we were created to be.

Satan asserted, "You will not surely die"—the first outright lie recorded in the Bible. It seconds Jesus' statement that Satan is the father of lies (John 8:44). It is easy to imagine the line of argumentation the serpent may have used. Eve could see for herself that the serpent was eating the fruit and was not dying. In fact, far from dying, the serpent was able to converse with her. If the fruit could effect such a dramatic change in a lowly serpent, just imagine what it could do for someone made in God's image! Such was the craftiness of the devil that he was able to move Eve to want to do what she knew God had told her not to do.

Here Eve made her second mistake: she listened when the serpent contradicted God. If she had thought about it, she would immediately have known that the serpent was an enemy of God and hence her enemy also. This lie was a warning to Eve that she was in danger, but she missed the warning. From this point on, the devil was in charge, leading her onward to her ruin.

The lie that disobedience doesn't bring death is still widely taught and believed. Many people hold that humans have an immortal, conscious soul that never dies. The soul, they assert, lives on after the body dies. Some think the soul goes either to heaven or hell, to live on for eternity. Others think the soul migrates through a series of other creatures in a never-ending cycle. And still others think the soul is a person's spirit that haunts the area where the person died. None of these ideas is biblical. All of them are derived from the first lie, "You will not surely die." The Bible teaches that God alone is immortal (1 Timothy 6:16), death is like an unconscious sleep, and the sleeping person is resurrected in an act of re-creation at the end of time (John 5:28, 29).[2]

Knowing good and evil

The prize the devil had promised that Eve would receive if she ate the forbidden fruit was the knowledge of good and evil. The quest for knowledge has had mixed results. Increased knowledge has brought a better understanding of the Bible and a much higher standard of living. But it has also brought problems. The ancient city of Athens was named for Athena, the goddess of wisdom and philosophy. The influence of Greek paganism continues to this day, to the detriment of true wisdom. The early Christian church had to deal with a philosophy named Gnosticism. This name is derived from the Greek word *gnosis,* which means "knowledge." Following in the path of the Greek philosophers in a movement known as the Enlightenment, eighteenth-century philosophers and thinkers looked to human wisdom for the solutions to human problems. Much of the scientific knowledge that has come because of these movements has been used to increase the efficiency with which humans manipulate or kill one another.

All these attempts to resolve human problems through reason apart from God have failed. Knowledge has indeed increased, but its misuse has greatly increased the wickedness of the race. Eve's decision to seek the knowledge of good and evil has resulted in much trouble and sorrow.

Eve was deceived by what she saw, and unfortunately, she chose to trust what she saw more than what God had told her. The text identifies three things she saw, each of which led her further down the road to the fatal ending. First, Eve saw that the tree was good for food. In fact, it may actually have appeared to be better than the fruit from the other trees of the Garden.

Second, she saw that the food was pleasant to the eyes. The Hebrew word translated "pleasant" (*ta'awah*) appears in the story of the quail in the wilderness as well (Numbers 11:31–34). In that story, many people died from eating the quail. The place where this happened was named, using the same Hebrew word, "graves of lust."[3]

And third, Eve saw that the tree was "desirable to make one wise." This phrase uses the same Hebrew word (*chamad*) as is seen in Exodus 20:17, "You shall not covet." The problem mentioned in both these passages is discontent with what one has and the desire for what is not legitimately available.

The temptation Eve faced didn't rest upon hearsay, but upon actual, observed physical evidence. Alas, humans are easily deceived by physical appearances. As with Eve, desire and lust often play a key role in what we think we see. History is replete with stories of deception in which people were led astray by appearances. Eve was merely the first to experience this.

The same temptations that came to Eve come to each of us. The apostle John warns us against these very things: "Do not love the world or the things in the world. If anyone loves the world, the love of the Father is not in him. For all that is in the world—the lust of the flesh, the lust of the eyes, and the pride of life—is not of the Father but is of the world. And the world is passing away, and the lust of it; but he who does the will of God abides forever" (1 John 2:15–17).

The three temptations John warned against are the very same temptations Eve faced. The desire for the fruit that was good for food corresponds with the lust of the flesh. The interest in the tree that was pleasant to the eyes corresponds with the lust of the eyes. And the desire for the "wisdom" to be gained by eating the fruit corresponds with the pride of life. We face temptation on these same points. John admonishes us not to repeat Eve's mistakes.

Dining with the devil

Eve chose to eat the forbidden fruit. It is true that she was deceived, but she was deceived because she disbelieved God. She knew that God had said they weren't to eat the fruit. She even told the serpent that God had forbidden it. But she became convinced by the appearances and the devil's argument that God wasn't telling the truth. She accepted the devil's lunch invitation and chose to eat from the menu he had prepared. Eating the fruit was Eve's fourth mistake, and it brought irrevocable consequences.

Eve then gave some fruit to Adam and he ate. When Eve brought Adam the fruit, he knew immediately what had happened. He wasn't deceived by the words of Satan (1 Timothy 2:14). He disobeyed, as did Eve, but his disobedience was worse because it was knowing, willful, and intentional. Adam was guilty of both disobedience and presumption. He knowingly disobeyed, presumptuously thinking that God would have to find a way to resolve the problem. This may be why Adam's sin is the one that the Bible writers mention when discussing the Fall (Romans 5:14; 1 Corinthians 15:22).

Jesus also invites us to eat with Him (Revelation 3:20), but His menu offers the bread of life rather than the knowledge of death Satan offered. All we need to do is accept His invitation.

Jesus was victorious over the same temptations that overcame Adam and Eve (Matthew 4:1–11). Eve was tempted by the lust of the flesh through appetite. Satan brought this temptation to Christ after He had fasted for forty days. Satan tempted Him to use His divine power to provide bread to satisfy His hunger, but Jesus said No.

Eve succumbed to the "lust of the eyes" temptation when she gave in to her desire for the beautiful but forbidden fruit. Satan brought this temptation to Jesus by showing Him the kingdoms of the world. He offered them to Jesus, asking in exchange that Jesus assert that Satan had the right to give the kingdoms to Him—which of course would have implied that they belonged to Satan.

Eve was overcome by the temptation of pride when she coveted the wisdom falsely promised. In contrast, Jesus refused to make a spectacular, prideful exhibit of jumping off the pinnacle of the temple.

Adam presumptuously ate of the fruit and tried to shift the responsibility for the consequences to the Creator, but Jesus refused to put God to the test. Jesus showed perfect trust in His heavenly Father, while Adam and Eve distrusted Him. In every point where Adam and Eve failed, Jesus overcame. Therefore, God can be just when He justifies those who believe in Him (Romans 3:26), so that, "as in Adam all die, even so in Christ all shall be made alive" (1 Corinthians 15:22).

From blessed to cursed

During Creation week, God pronounced blessings on what He had made. The entrance of sin brought curses instead. The "ground" that was cursed included more than just the soil minerals; it also included the plants, and Adam and Eve also felt the effects themselves. The serpent was cursed more than the rest of the animals, which implies that the curse was broadly applied and not confined to the serpent alone. Indeed, it seems the entire world was affected by the curses (Romans 8:20–22).

Sin affected the entire creation, including humans. The image of God was defaced, and we humans no longer have the relationship to the rest of creation God created us to have.

One example of the defacing of the image of God is in the exercise of dominion.[4] Adam was charged with tending and guarding the Garden and bringing the entire earth under his management. Today we see this responsibility abused in many ways. Earth has enough resources to sustain life indefinitely. But humans have been careless and wasteful in their use of the land, exploiting its resources with unsustainable greed. The harmony of the original creation has been replaced by antagonistic relationships, abundant pests, and violent predators. Virulent diseases disable unnumbered multitudes of humans and other creatures, and they bring suffering and death. All these things are the result of sin, which has damaged how humans exercise their dominion over the other creatures, distorting the image of God that the humans were meant to display.

Human morality is another aspect of the image of God that has been defaced by sin. As Jesus illustrated in His life, unselfish service to others is central to the image of God in humans. But this is not often seen among us today. Instead, our relationships are dominated by self-interest. Rich and poor alike take advantage of each other, using every available strategy of coercion, dishonesty, and deceit. Violence is common; the judicial and political systems are corrupt; business practices are dishonest; and the public has little tolerance for truth and goodness. The moral aspects of the image of God have become so corrupted that many deny that humans ever were created in God's image.

Sociability is a third feature of the image of God that shows the damaging effects of sin. Marriage was intended to be a great blessing, the foundation of happy families and stable societies, but it has often become a curse. Spousal conflict, marital unfaithfulness, unwanted and neglected children, and casual divorce are too often the case. Not only marriage, but all social relationships have suffered. Humans are separated from each other by tribalism and social status, and they are separated from God by overt rebellion. In many people, the image of God is scarcely discernible because it has been so badly defaced.

A fourth dimension of the image of God that sin has damaged is the cycle of work and rest. God set the pattern of six days of labor and a day of rest, and He has called humans to follow His example (Exodus 20:8–11).[5] But few do. People commonly suffer from fatigue due to overwork. And most of those who do recognize a day of rest do so on a day other than that chosen by God, and few devote the entire day to worship and spiritual renewal. Even those who observe the seventh day of the Commandments find it easy to forget its sacred status. This aspect of the image of God has been defaced by sin to the point where those who observe the seventh-day Sabbath are often held in contempt by other people.

As a result of their sin, both Adam and Eve eventually died. Satan told them they wouldn't die, but he lied. They were made from dust, and to dust they returned. The Bible says, "Altogether, Adam lived 930 years, and then he died" (Genesis 5:2, NIV). We aren't told when Eve died, but we know that both Adam and Eve witnessed death. Their son Cain killed his brother Abel. Since that time, with only two known exceptions, Enoch and Elijah, every person who has ever lived has eventually died. But while death is a feared and relentless enemy, it is preferable to a never-ending life of sin.

Death is not the work of God, but of Satan. The Creator's will is that His creatures should have life (John 10:10; cf. Revelation 4:11), but Satan was a murderer from the beginning (John 8:4). When he incited Adam and Eve to sin, he assumed some of the responsibility for the death that resulted. But Jesus came to destroy Satan's power of death (Hebrews 2:14), and He overcame him, providing a new life for all who would accept it.

Conclusion

God created Adam and Eve in His image, placed them in a privileged environment, and gave them instructions on how to preserve the goodness of creation. Despite the advantages they had, they distrusted God and chose to disobey Him. Eve was deceived by Satan; nevertheless, when she ate the forbidden fruit, she knew that she was disobeying God. Adam was not deceived; he willfully chose to disobey. The sins of Adam and Eve brought Satan's influence into the world. And Satan brought death, and he defaced the image of God in humans. But Christ overcame Satan on every point on which Adam and Eve failed, and He has provided a way to restore all that was lost because of sin.

---

1. See also John 8:44, where Jesus identifies the devil as the father of lies and a murderer "from the beginning."

2. Cf. 1 Corinthians 15:51–54; 1 Thessalonians 4:15–17.

3. Numbers 11:34: *kibroth hatta' awah*, or "graves of desire."

4. See chapter 10 of this book.

5. Cf. Exodus 31:12–18; Mark 2:27.

CHAPTER 7

Evil in the Creation

During Creation week, God pronounced blessings on what He created, and at the end of the week, God said that it was all "very good." The picture is of a world without predatory violence, suffering, or death. But this is not the world in which we live. Violence, pain, and suffering are so familiar that many people find it difficult to imagine a world without them. Evil casts a shadow over nature, reducing our ability to understand it rightly. We don't see clearly, but "in a mirror, dimly" (1 Corinthians 13:12). How did such dramatic changes occur?

Sin's sentences

The sentence on the serpent. After Adam and Eve's confession (Genesis 3:12, 13), God pronounced sentences on all of those involved in humankind's first sins. He directed the first sentence to the serpent. It was cursed "more than all cattle, and more than every beast of the field" (Genesis 3:14). This seems to imply that though the curse would change the serpent the most, it would affect all the cattle and beasts of the field. But whether or not the text was meant to say the sentence applied to the entire animal kingdom, it *is* clear that the effects of sin do extend to all animals (Romans 8:20).

As a result of the curse, the serpent was to go on its belly and eat dust. This may have a double meaning. First, it meant that there would be changes to the anatomy of the serpent so that it would crawl upon its belly. This implies that it previously had some other means of locomotion, such as legs or wings. Biologists recognize that the ancestors of the snakes that exist now had limbs, and that the changes snakes have undergone involve changes in the genes that control embryological development. Second, the curse may also imply that Satan himself, the real "serpent" in the story, would "eat the dust"—a metaphor pointing to eventual destruction.

It's likely that the curse included the potential for genetic changes not only in snakes, but in all other animals as well. We infer that animals changed, some of them developing the anatomy needed to support a mode of existence dependent upon violence and predation, and others adapting to a life of parasitism. The substantial changes required means that we can't assume that the animals we see now look or act the same as the animals that existed before sin.

Lest Satan have complete control over humanity, God would help them to resist temptation by putting enmity between the serpent and the woman. Humans would dislike evil. And though Satan would inflict suffering, the bruising of the heel, in the end he would be defeated: his head would be crushed (Genesis 3:15). Sin and evil will eventually end, but at a cost.[1]

The sentence on the woman. The second sentence was pronounced on the woman. Her family relationships would be affected, and childbirth would be painful. The phrase "your desire shall be for your husband" (Genesis 3:16) may reflect the fact that the harmony of the couple would be disrupted.[2] To preserve the marriage institution, which was so important for the welfare of the race, her husband would rule[3] over her. Unfortunately, in the fallen world, the husband and wife may have conflicting ideas of what that leadership should be. When we observe the difficulties that those who are married experience, we should remember we are fallen creatures, and we should strive to restore the ideal harmonious marriage relationship intended by the Creator.

The sentence on the man. The first part of the man's sentence was that his life would be one of toil and sorrow (Genesis 3:17–19). The work required of him would be strenuous, enough to cause him to sweat. The work man must do would increase because the ground was cursed and would now produce thorns and thistles. The implication here is that thorns and thistles didn't exist prior to this time.*

The curse also brought about a change in diet. Humans would now eat herbaceous plants along with the fruits and seeds originally provided. In Genesis 2, the creation of humans is depicted as occurring before certain types of plants existed. Two types of plants are mentioned in this context: the "plant of the field"[4] and the "herb of the field."[5] Some scholars of Hebrew suggest these expressions may refer, respectively, to the wild shrubs of arid regions and to the cultivated herbs, both of which were subject to changes because of the curses.[6] If this interpretation is correct, it is another example of the kinds of changes that have taken place in plants since Creation.

Adam's sentence includes death. After a life of toil and sorrow, he would die. He was taken from the dust, and he would return to the dust. This part of the sentence wasn't imposed immediately, but it would happen in due time. In grace, Adam was given the chance to live a probationary life, demonstrating by his actions and attitudes whether he would accept the gift God was offering in the promise of the victory of the "Seed."

The darkening of the "glass"

Adam had been given dominion over the creatures of the sea, sky, and land, and had been given the work of gardening. All of these were affected by the curses sin brought. In fact, the entire world was affected by the curses (Romans 8:20–22). Not only was the good creation marred by sin and the curses, but the human mind itself has suffered damage. It has been darkened, making it resistant to the truth God has revealed both in nature and in His Word. Jeremiah describes the human mind as "deceitful above all things, and desperately wicked" (Jeremiah 17:9). People even willingly forget that it was God who created the earth and everything in it (2 Peter 3:5, 6). Sin has made such a deep divide between us—created beings—and the Creator that, without divine enlightenment, we read nature incorrectly.[7]

Despite the distortion of God's good creation by the destructive power of sin, there have always been some who can see design in nature and probably

---

* Biologists tell us that thorns are produced by genetic changes that altered the development of what should have become leaves. Sin has caused both plants and animals to experience changes in their developmental genetics.

some who deny it. Advances in science have added to the evidence pertaining to this question, and it remains a topic of active discussion today.[8]

In fact, the question of design in nature is one of the great issues of all time. The ancient Greek philosophers discussed it.[9] Theologians and philosophers of the Enlightenment argued about it.[10] And the debate between theists, who affirm design in nature, and materialists, who deny it, continues today.[11]

The view that nature gives evidence of design has two branches, which aren't necessarily mutually exclusive. They are the argument *to* design and the argument *from* design.

The argument to design starts with the premise that nature appears orderly and exhibits features that indicate design by some intelligence. It then concludes that nature truly must have been designed by some intelligent mind. This argument focuses on design itself and doesn't attempt to identify the designer. The intelligent design group uses this argument.[12]

The second argument starts where the first one ends. Its premise is that nature is designed, and it concludes that the Designer is the God of the Bible. These two arguments are closely related and are often—but not necessarily always—linked.

While most Christians and other monotheists would recognize design and attribute it to the biblical Creator, others would not. Pantheists might accept the idea that nature is designed, but they would propose a different designer—perhaps a universal spirit present in all matter or a mysterious force that causes matter to organize itself. Materialists deny both the argument to design and the argument from design.

Steven Weinberg, winner of the 1979 Nobel Prize in physics, sees too much evil in nature to believe anyone designed the universe. He explains: "It is almost irresistible to imagine that all this beauty was somehow laid on for our benefit. But the God of birds and trees would have to be also the God of birth defects and cancer."[13]

The design argument would be much more convincing if it weren't for the problem of evil.

The problem of "natural evil"

"Natural evil" is the term used to designate suffering caused by forces of nature that humans can't control. The existence of natural evil is the principal objection to the argument from design. The evil that humans cause isn't much of a problem; people universally recognize it as the responsibility of those humans who cause it. But who is responsible for the suffering caused by natural disasters such as floods, tsunamis, earthquakes, tornadoes, droughts, and so on? People answer this question in different ways, depending on how they view the relationship between God and the world.

For the materialist who denies the existence of God, natural evil is just natural; there's nothing to explain. Earthquakes happen, and people are killed—along with cockroaches and rats.

To the believer in God, natural evil is the result of a combination of factors. God is certainly capable of preventing natural evil, but He respects the choice humans have made to follow Satan, so He limits His intervention. Meanwhile, Satan is actively working to destroy everything he can of God's handiwork. To the extent God permits, Satan works to cause natural disasters (Job 1; 2). He would undoubtedly do more if he could. Believers recognize that sin gave Satan access to the world, and natural evil is one of the results.

Some people believe that God causes evil because He is angry with sinners and wants to exact revenge on them for their ingratitude. It may have been this belief that explains why people commonly call natural disasters "acts of God."

Others believe that God is indifferent to human suffering—that He simply doesn't care what happens. Those who deny the existence and power of Satan often struggle to believe there is a good God who cares about them. They can see the evidence for design, but they cannot reconcile the idea of a Divine Designer with the presence of natural evil. This leads us to consider the role of supernatural agents in causing natural evil.

When Adam and Eve sinned, they allowed evil into the world. Their disobedience called for a response from God, which was given in the form of curses and the sentence of death.[14] God responded by establishing limits to the effects of sin, by reminding humans of their dependence on Him, and by providing hope for the future. People might consider this response to involve a form of evil,[15] but God intended it to be redemptive (Deuteronomy 8:5; Hebrews 12:5–7).

Sin brought evil in a destructive form. When Satan deceived Adam and Eve, evil gained a foothold in the world. Satan didn't intend the evil he brought to redeem humanity—to move them toward a positive relationship with God. Rather, he meant it to separate them from God forever. Thus, there are two streams of "evil" flowing through our world, one intended to bring us back to God and one intended to separate us from Him forever. This complicates our understanding of natural evil.

It isn't clear whether the curses God pronounced upon the earth were imposed immediately or whether they were predictive of what would eventually happen. One may also wonder whether they were imposed by God directly, or whether God gave Satan freedom to distort the beauty of the original creation. Perhaps both are true.

One view is that God reduced the extent of His protective care, permitting us to see for ourselves how sin affects creation. This might be what Paul had in mind when he wrote, "The creation was subjected to futility, not willingly, but because of Him who subjected it in hope" (Romans 8:20). And God may have used the curses He pronounced to modify creation so that it could cope with the effects of sin and death.

On the other hand, Satan's ability to influence nature must not be underestimated. He is able to bring fire down from heaven and to cause tornadoes (Job 1:16, 19). He can bring disease (Job 2:7; Luke 13:16) and appear in various disguises (2 Corinthians 11:14).[16] And the parable of the tares implies that he also corrupts the plants (Matthew 13:24–30). He claims to be the ruler of this world,[17] a claim that even Jesus recognized (John 14:30).[18]

These two possibilities—that the curses on the earth were implemented by God or by Satan—may both be true. Both God and Satan are active in the world, and both may bring experiences we regard as evil.

Seeing God in nature

Many biblical texts affirm that God acts in nature. The psalmists could see God's power and wisdom in nature: in a thunderstorm (Psalm 29), in the raging of the sea (Psalm 93), and in the structure of the creation (Psalm 104). To the believer, God's glory and wisdom can be seen throughout the creation. David famously wrote, "The heavens declare the glory of God" (Psalm 19:1). Looking at the stars, he was reminded of their Creator, whose glory was manifested in the consistency with which He maintained the order seen in the sky. The same point is made in Psalm 8, where David expressed his wonder at the fact that the great God who created the heavens would take such an interest in humans.

But what of the unbeliever?

Even those who don't know God can see evidence of His existence in the things He has created. When, in his travels, the apostle Paul contended with pagans, he sometimes used the evidence in nature to argue for God's existence. When speaking to the pagans in Lystra, for instance, he spoke of the rains and the harvest seasons as evidence of the Creator God (Acts 14:15–17). When addressing the philosophers on Mars' Hill, he pointed to their acknowledgment of the existence of an "unknown god," he showed that there is a Creator God unknown to them (Acts 17:22–34), and he then called upon them to worship Him. To the Romans, Paul wrote that the witness of the creation is available to all, but he wasn't optimistic about our ability to see God in nature (Romans 1:19, 20). Specifically, he said that "what may be known of God" are "His eternal power and Godhead." From nature, anyone can infer that a Creator God exists, that He is powerful, and that He is eternal. This is sufficient to make every person accountable to God.

One evidence of God's goodness that appeals to everyone is a faithful, generous believer. Those who faithfully observe God's laws are giving a witness that reaches those who aren't acquainted with the law (Deuteronomy 4:5, 6). Jesus identified the two greatest commandments: we are to love God supremely, and we are to love our neighbor as ourselves (Matthew 22:34–40). If the problem of evil is the biggest hindrance to belief in God, a life of loving service may well be the strongest evidence of His existence.

Conclusion

The sin of Adam and Eve brought changes to every part of the world. It gave Satan access to the world, which has resulted in untold misery and suffering. The blessing God pronounced on the original creation has been overprinted by curses on the animals, the plants, and the land itself. The image of God that humankind bore has been defaced, and the human mind has been darkened so that it no longer perceives clearly the presence of God in creation.

Yet God has not left us without evidence of His existence and power. We can see these attributes clearly in the things He has made. But there is a better and clearer witness to His goodness and love: it is seen in the lives of those who, following the example of Jesus, live to serve others. Jesus called Himself "the light of the world" (John 8:12), and He called on His followers to be the same (Matthew 5:14–16). Above all, it is this light that is needed to relieve the darkness of humankind's minds.

---

1. See chapter 12 of this book.

2. White, EG. *Patriarchs and Prophets*. Nampa, ID: Pacific Press® (2002), 58; cf. Collins, CJ. *Genesis 1–4: A Linguistic, Literary, and Theological Commentary*. Phillipsburg, NJ: P&R Publishing (2006), 159, 160.

3. Hebrew *masal;* note this is different from man's "rule" (Hebrew *rada*) over the animals in Genesis 1:26–28; see Davidson, R. *Flame of Yahweh: Sexuality in the Old Testament*. Peabody, MA: Hendrickson (2007), chapter 2.

4. Genesis 2:5; Hebrew *siach hassadeh,* "shrub of the field."

5. Genesis 2:5; Hebrew *'eseb hassadeh,* "herb of the field."

6. Younker, RW. "Genesis 2: A Second Creation Account?" in JT. Baldwin, ed., *Creation, Catastrophe, and Calvary*. Hagerstown, MD: Review and Herald® (2000), 69–78.

7. White, EG. "Man's Failure to Interpret Nature." *Testimonies for the Church*, vol. 8. Mountain View, CA: Pacific Press® (1948), 257, 258; cf. Romans 1:21–23.

8. E.g., see Behe, MJ. *Darwin's Black Box*. NY: Free Press (1996); Meyer, SC. *Signature in the Cell*. NY: Harper One (2009).

9. Design was affirmed by Plato, Cicero, and others, but denied by Leucippus, Lucretius, and others.

10. Thomas Aquinas and William Paley famously affirmed design, while David Hume is its most famous opponent.

11. Major supporters of design include William Dembski and Michael Behe, while opponents include Richard Dawkins and the late Stephen Jay Gould.

12. E.g., see Dembski, WA. and JM. Kushiner. *Signs of Intelligence*. Grand Rapids, MI: Brazos Press (2001).

13. Weinberg, S. *Dreams of a Final Theory*. New York: Vintage Books (1992), 250.

14. Bauer, S. " 'Dying You Shall Die': The Meaning of Genesis 2:17," *Ministry* 83/12(December 2011):6–9.

15. Hebrew *ra',* "evil" or "bad"; Exodus 7–12; Deuteronomy 28:15, 68; Isaiah 45:7.

16. Cf. Genesis 3:1; 1 Samuel 28:3–14.

17. Implied in Job 1:6, 7; Job 2:1, 2; Isaiah 14:16, 17; explicit in Matthew 4:8, 9.

18. Cf. John 12:31; John 16:11.

CHAPTER 8

Creation and Providence

Many people wonder how much God is really doing in our world. Some see Him only in catastrophes, such as earthquakes, tornadoes, and floods. Others see Him as too distant to be involved and doubt the reality of miracles, attributing every event to "the forces of nature."

"Providence" refers to how God governs the world. We commonly think of providence as an act of God in answer to prayer. It does have to do with answers to prayer, but it is broader than that. The Bible portrays God as actively involved in providing for His creatures. God acts through both special acts of providence, such as answering prayer, and through general providence, such as sustaining the processes of nature. In this chapter, we'll examine some aspects of God's governance of the world, including general and special providence.

General providence

At the end of Creation week, God rested from His work of creating (Genesis 2:2, 3). He wasn't resting because He was tired, but because He had completed the task. God is no longer creating as He did during Creation week, but this doesn't mean that He is inactive. Jesus said, "My Father has been working until now, and I have been working" (John 5:17). God has not abandoned the world. He still works in it.

God's general providence was set in place at Creation. As God was creating the universe, He established the patterns, the "laws," by which He would govern it. As part of His work of creating, He provided the necessities of life. To be suitable for living organisms, their environment must have light, oxygen, fresh water, dry land, and environmental cues[1] so that the organisms can develop regular behavior patterns. God made all of these during Creation week, and He maintains them through His general providence.

God's general providence is exercised through what we call "the laws of nature." These "laws" aren't requirements that restrict God's activity; rather, they are tools He has chosen to accomplish His will. We could call them "the laws of providence" because they aren't inherent properties of the physical universe, but are instead patterns of governance freely chosen by the Creator for the purpose of sustaining the universe He has created.

God is the source of nature's laws. The structure of the universe is based on matter and energy, which are interchangeable. Matter is sustained in existence by what are called the "fundamental forces." These include the force of gravity and the forces that hold atoms together.[2] Scientists describe these forces as "fundamental properties of matter." As believers, we recognize that matter has no properties of its own. God established the properties of matter by His own will. We can consider the fundamental forces to be God's power continuously exercised to maintain the existence of the matter of the universe.[3]

Since the Fall, God has had to deal with a damaged creation. He has chosen to fix it rather than to discard it. This means He continues to sustain it even in its damaged condition. He even maintains the existence of the atoms and molecules that make up the bodies of those who oppose His will and who would destroy Him if they could.

God's general providence includes maintaining the conditions needed to sustain life. After the great Flood, God promised Noah that the seasonal and daily cycles would continue (Genesis 8:22). God brings the wind, the rain, and the sunshine for His creatures—for all of them, the good and the bad alike (Psalms 135:7; 145:15, 16; Matthew 5:45). Similarly, He provides food for both the cattle and the lion (Psalm 104:14, 21). The thorns and thistles benefit from His provision as certainly as do the grapevines and fruit trees. But we shouldn't interpret the fact that He supplies each of these with the necessities of life as His endorsement of them in their fallenness. Instead, it is an example of how God cares even for His enemies, just as He calls us to do (Matthew 5:43–48).

God's providence may be creative. The psalmist praises the way in which God formed his inward parts while he was still in the womb (Psalm 139:13). This refers to the process of development—that marvelous growth of a single cell into a new person who bears the image of God. We consider that God created us, although He didn't do so in the same way that He created Adam and Eve. God isn't still doing the work He completed during Creation week, but He is sustaining the processes by which new individuals are produced. He also uses the same laws of nature to bring health and healing, so that the psalmist is correct when he says that God "heals all your diseases" (Psalm 103:3)—even when He uses processes we would regard as "natural."

General providence refers to the divine governance of the world through the regular processes we call "natural laws." These laws allow things to go wrong. Hence, in our world of sin, we have floods and droughts, disease and death. To the person who doesn't know of the world to come, the evil that people experience in this world can sometimes make existence seem pointless. But those who know God's promises look forward to the "new heavens and a new earth in which righteousness dwells" (2 Peter 3:13).

Special providence

In addition to governing nature through "natural laws," God also acts within the universe to cause specific events. We can consider these events as miracles because we don't know of any potential explanation for them in terms of the regularities we usually see. By definition, miracles are rare. We consider events that are predictable to be natural phenomena and not miracles. If all the dead were resurrected at every full moon, we would likely come to regard that to involve some law of nature regardless of whether we could explain it.

Special providence may be carried out directly, by an act of God, or it may be carried out indirectly. The raising of Lazarus is an example of special providence through a direct act of God (John 11:38–44). God's power acted directly on Lazarus's body, giving it life. Jesus' healing of the son of the nobleman of Capernaum was another act of special providence through direct action (John 4:46–54). Even though Jesus was in Cana, several miles away from the nobleman's home in Capernaum, it is classified as an instance of direct action because the sick boy was healed at Jesus' command. God acted directly to return the boy to health.

Often—perhaps even most of the time—miracles occur indirectly, as when God used a wind to bring quail to the Israelites (Numbers 11:31–34). God didn't create them on the spot or make them disappear from their habitat and reappear in the camp of the Israelites; He used the wind to transport the quail there. However, as in this case, a miracle accomplished through indirect means still involves a direct act by God that starts the chain of events. How else would one explain the arrival of so many quail in the interior of the Arabian Peninsula shortly after God told the people He was going to supply them with meat? God must have acted directly to bring the wind at the right time and place to gather the quail and carry them to the place He chose. This event was an act of special providence brought about indirectly, through a chain of circumstances initiated by a direct divine act.

Very often, an act of special providence is accompanied by some human activity that in itself wouldn't accomplish the desired effect but that fulfilled a condition God said must be met before He would act. An example is the healing of Naaman from his leprosy (2 Kings 5:9–14). Through Elisha, God instructed Naaman to wash in the Jordan River seven times. When Naaman did, he was healed. Surely, there was nothing in the water of that river that healed Naaman; the healing was a direct act of God. Yet the water played an important part in the miracle, and if Naaman had refused to follow the instructions, he wouldn't have been healed. We could call this a kind of conditional special providence— a divine act that occurs only with human cooperation.

Scripture contains many other examples of conditional special providence; among them, the freshening of the bitter water at Marah when Moses, following God's command, felled a tree and threw it in the water (Exodus 15:22–25); the healing of those who looked in faith at the bronze serpent (Numbers 21:4–9); the rain that came in answer to Elijah's prayer (1 Kings 18:41–46); the oil that continued to flow until all the vessels the widow collected were full (2 Kings 4:1–7); and the changing of water to wine at the wedding in Cana when the jars were filled and taken to the host (John 2:1–10).

God sometimes acts in ways He wouldn't have to in an unfallen world. Thus the Bible sometimes pictures God as bringing disasters that destroy multitudes of people to punish their rebellion. The Genesis Flood is the first and most drastic example in Scripture, but there are many more. The plagues of Egypt (Exodus 7–12) were singular acts of providence that gained the release of the Hebrew slaves from Egypt, but at the cost of much of Egypt's resources. Similarly, the destruction of the cities of Sodom and Gomorrah (Genesis 19), the opening of the earth to swallow Korah, Dathan, and Abiram (Numbers 16:28–33), the killing of Uzzah when he touched the ark (2 Samuel 6:6, 7), and the destruction of the Assyrian army in the siege of Jerusalem (2 Kings 19:35) were intended to preserve the agencies through which God intended to make salvation available to humankind.

Special providence may be constructive or destructive, conditional or unconditional, direct or indirect, but it is always intended to be redemptive, while preserving free will. Eventually, the greatest providences of all time—the incarnation, death, and resurrection of Jesus—came, and these events were clearly redemptive.

Creation, providence, and the character of the Creator

Throughout the Bible, God is presented as omnipotent, merciful, and good. He provides for His people's needs; He protects them against harm; He guides and blesses in their plans; He cares for the needy as well as the wealthy. Still, questions sometimes arise about what kind of God He is. In today's society, many have accepted the theory that humans and animals have evolved from a common ancestor, yet they are skeptical that this could happen purely by chance and natural law. One result of this thinking is the theory that God is the Creator, but He used evolution as the method of creation. This proposal raises some very serious questions about the character of the Creator, and because the theory is quite popular in some parts of Christendom, it is worth commenting on here.

People use several different terms, such as "theistic evolution" or "evolutionary creation" or "providential evolution," to identify the theory that God used evolutionary processes to create. Regardless of the name chosen, such theories imply that God is evil. I will discuss six ways in which theories of evolutionary creation impugn the character of God. Readers can find a more comprehensive discussion in other sources.[4]

Evolutionary processes involve three steps that are inconsistent with God's character as revealed in the life and teachings of Jesus. These steps are competition due to limited resources, elimination of the weak by the stronger, and gradual improvement of the species. These steps raise at least six objections to the theory of evolutionary creation.

1. The theory of evolutionary creation implies that God intentionally limits resources so that there isn't enough for all. Evolution is based on competition due to limited resources. It's true that competition is unavoidable in our fallen world and that it entails suffering. But there are no limits on what the God that the Bible pictures can provide, and He works to relieve suffering. Jesus showed the generosity of God by ministering to all who were in need, and He showed the unlimited resources of God when He multiplied the loaves and fishes to feed the thousands who had gathered to hear Him teach (Matthew 14:13–21; 15:32–38). The limited resources element of the evolutionary creation theory mimics Satan's suggestion to Eve that God has withheld something from her. God doesn't cause shortages of resources; rather, they are the result of Satan's activities.

2. The theory of evolutionary creation implies that God approves the destruction of weaker individuals by those that are stronger. But the God of the Bible is the God of the living (Matthew 22:32). Jesus came to bring life (John 10:10), not death. Care for the poor is one of the primary requirements those who would follow God must meet, and those who don't provide such care face His condemnation (Matthew 25:31–46). It is Satan who is the "god" of death (Hebrews 2:14).

3. The theory that God used evolution as the process of creation also implies that He used an evil process to produce humans in His own

image, which Scripture claims is good. Many people have asked why God would use evil to create life forms rather than creating them directly Himself. One answer is that He wasn't able to accomplish what He wanted to all at once, so He had to do it in stages. But this can't be true because according to Scripture, God is omnipotent. An alternate explanation might be that He chose to create through an evolutionary process because He is indifferent to pain. But this can't be true either, because He is a God of love and mercy. Thus, the theory that God chose to use evolution to create can't be reconciled with His character.

4. Another problem with the theory of evolutionary creation is that it implies that God sets a higher moral standard for His creatures than He Himself follows. God has instructed us to be kind and merciful, to care for the weak and poor, and to serve others even at a cost to ourselves. But these requirements are inconsistent with the methods of evolutionary creation. If we're to follow the example set by a God who operates on the basis of evolutionary creation (Matthew 5:48), then we would support the efforts to weed out the genetically inferior for the good of the race, a process called eugenics. The results of such thinking can be seen in the history of the Nazis.[5]

5. The seventh-day Sabbath is another casualty of the implications of evolutionary creation. If there were no six days of creation, there cannot be a seventh-day Sabbath, because the seventh day is defined as the day that follows the six creation days. Evolutionary creationists can still keep every seventh day, of course, and they can justify their practice any way they wish, but their choice would be arbitrary. There is no logical connection between evolutionary creation and worship on the seventh day. This may not matter for those who keep a different day of the week anyway, but it does matter to those who choose to follow the fourth commandment (Exodus 20:8–11). Some people may point to Deuteronomy 5, where the reason given for keeping the Sabbath is the deliverance of Israel from Egypt, but this applies only to the Jews and doesn't provide any basis for determining which day is the seventh day. Evolutionary creation is quite compatible with regarding any day—or no day—as holy.

6. Finally, evolutionary creation denies the relationship between sin

and death. In the evolutionary interpretation of the fossil record, animals were suffering and dying long before humans came into existence. Evolutionary creation theory also denies that sin has any effect on nature. Evolutionists point out that the fossil record contains evidences of suffering and death similar to what we see in the world today. This view implies that the Bible writers got it wrong—Jesus didn't die for our sins, but for some other reason.

To explain the difference between humans and animals, many theistic evolutionists postulate that God chose two individuals and gave them immortal souls, conveying moral status on the "Adam" and "Eve" He thus created. But Scripture denies that *any* humans have immortal souls, saying that God alone has immortality (1 Timothy 6:15, 16) and that the redeemed will be given immortality only at the resurrection (1 Corinthians 15:52–54).

Whether called "evolutionary creation" or "theistic evolution," the theory that God chose evolutionary processes as His method of creation is false. It isn't compatible with the biblical story of Creation, the Fall, and salvation; it undermines the gospel; and it justifies the dual errors of Sunday worship (Daniel 7:25) and soul immortality (2 Corinthians 11:14).[6] The Bible tells the true story of Creation, accurately picturing in its pages the righteous character of God, the fallen nature of humans, and the gospel story, which are also verified by the life and teachings of Jesus.

Conclusion

Jesus is not only the Creator, but He is also the One who governs the world through His providence. He has made abundant provision for the needs of all His creatures by establishing the properties of the physical environment and the ecological relationships of living organisms. And although Adam's sin gave Satan access to this world and he now attempts to disrupt the systems God established at Creation and thus cause suffering and death, Jesus continues to maintain those divinely appointed systems.

In addition to the general provisions God established in the laws of nature that He put in place at Creation, God also from time to time works through acts of special providence to carry out His plan of redemption. These acts often appear to us as coincidences and sometimes as miracles, often in answer to prayer. Through these acts of special providence, God continues to care for the creation and to direct events to the culmination foretold in Scripture, when all things will be restored. A correct understanding of providence reveals the Creator to be all knowing and omnipotent. He is also merciful and good, qualities He wants His followers to develop as well.

---

1. Some microorganisms can survive without some of these features, but all sentient organisms require them.

2. These include the strong nuclear force and the electroweak force (the weak nuclear force and the electromagnetic force).

3. See White, EG. "Laws of Nature," *Testimonies for the Church,* vol. 8. Mountain View, CA: Pacific Press® (1948), 259–261.

4. Richards, J, ed. *God and Evolution.* Seattle: Discovery Institute Press (2010); Hunter, CG. *Darwin's God.* Grand Rapids, MI: Brazos Press (2001); Baldwin, JT, ed. *Creation, Catastrophe, and Calvary.* Hagerstown, MD: Review and Herald® (2000).

5. Bergman, J. "Darwinism and the Nazi Race Holocaust," *Creation Ex Nihilo Technical Journal* 13/2(1999):101–111; see also Weikart, R. *From Darwin to Hitler: Evolutionary Ethics, Eugenics, and Racism in Germany.* NY: Palgrave Macmillan (2006).

6. See also Ezekiel 18:4; Isaiah 8:19, 20.

CHAPTER 9

Creation and Marriage

The family is the fundamental unit of society, and marriage is the basis of family. What the marriage is, the family becomes, and what the family is, the society becomes. When family relationships are respected and honored as they should be, society will be characterized by mutual respect and honorable behavior. Few themes of practical living are as important as marriage and family relationships. Our view of marriage is inextricably linked with our view of origins.[1]

In the Creation narrative of Genesis 1 and 2, the entire creation is described as "good"—all except for one thing, it was not good for the man to be alone (Genesis 2:18). Loneliness is so undesirable that judicial systems sometimes use it as the ultimate punishment short of execution. Millions of people suffer from loneliness, and it makes perfect sense that God would declare the situation "not good." The image of God includes a strong component of relationship.

Adam realized his lack of companionship when God brought the animals to him to be named. As he saw the animals coming in pairs, he felt the need for a companion for himself. This need God proceeded to supply. He arranged the first marriage, and in doing so, established a pattern for all the marriages that followed.

When Adam was aware of his need for companionship, God caused him to go into a deep sleep, removed a rib from his side, and used it to "build"[2] a woman. Notice that the woman was God's idea. Adam had no part in the design and construction of his companion. If he had, he might reasonably have considered himself to be the owner of the woman. But God is the Creator and Owner of both the man and the woman—a point He hasn't left in doubt.

The method God chose to use in creating the woman has meaning for the marriage relationship. The woman was made from a rib, a bone that covers the heart. If she had been made from a bone of the foot, the ancients would have interpreted this to mean women were meant to be dominated by men. If she had been made from a bone of Adam's head, women might have been considered superior to men. But neither of these was the case. Eve was intended to be a companion for Adam, to work together with him, and to cover and protect his heart. And, in turn, he would nurture and protect her.

Note also that like the man, the woman was created individually. As an individual, she was personally accountable to God in the same way Adam was. Both individuals were endowed with the image of God, which included free will. Eve's relationship to Adam would be one of equality regardless of the roles each undertook in the marriage.

God created the woman to be a "helper" (ʿezer; Genesis 2:18) for Adam. One might wonder if this verse means that the woman was intended to work for the man as his servant, but this is not the meaning of the Hebrew word translated "helper." Many biblical texts use the same word to refer to the help the Lord gives people. For example, Moses invoked God to be a help against the enemies of Israel. In his farewell blessing to the Israelites, Moses refers to God, who "rides the heavens to *help* you" and who is "the shield of your *help*" (Deuteronomy 33:26, 29; emphasis added). And the psalmist states, "My *help* comes from the LORD, who made heaven and earth" (Psalm 121:2; emphasis added). From these and many other biblical examples, we can infer that Eve was created to participate with Adam in the activities of life. She was not to be a servant, but someone on whom he could depend for help and support, someone who could share the responsibilities with him. Proverbs 31 is a beautiful description of such a woman.

God intended the man and the woman to carry out together the mandate that He, their Creator, had given them. This included expressing the image of God in tasks such as the production of children, the filling and subduing of the world, and the management of the other creatures (Genesis 1:27, 28). Not only did Adam need Eve's help to fulfill this mandate, but her companionship would increase the joy he would get from carrying out the tasks.

After creating Eve, God brought her to Adam. He was so pleased that he expressed his joy in poetry—the first poem ever composed by a human.

> "This is now bone of my bones
> And flesh of my flesh;
> She shall be called Woman,
> Because she was taken out of Man" (Genesis 2:23).[3]

This poem reminds us of another poem in the Creation account, this one about the creation of Adam and Eve.

> So God created man in His own image,
> in the image of God He created him;
> male and female He created them (Genesis 1:27).

These are the only two places in the Creation narrative where poetry is used.[4] This fact surely must have some meaning for the significance of the creation of the man and the woman. It certainly expresses joy at the creation of the ones gifted with God's own image.

The marriage covenant

Marriage is a covenant—an agreement between two parties (Proverbs 2:17; Malachi 2:14). We may take the Lord's command regarding marriage (Mark 10:6–9; quoting Genesis 1:27; 2:24) as expressing the content of the marriage covenant. It sets forth at least three clauses. The first is that the man should "leave his father and mother." Many a home has been wrecked due to failure on this point. A man who is not prepared to live independently of his father and mother is not ready for marriage. Only God holds a higher place in the hearts of those who are married than does their spouse.

The second clause of the marriage covenant is that the man should "be joined to his wife" (Genesis 2:24). The Hebrew verb here, *dabaq,* means "to adhere to," "to stay close to." This word is also used in other contexts—for instance, in Moses' command to "hold fast" to the Lord (Deuteronomy 10:20; cf. 11:22; 13:4; 30:20), and in the statement that Ruth "clung to" Naomi (Ruth 1:14). When we marry, we must not only leave our father and mother, we must also "cling" to our marriage partner. The marriage covenant applies "for better, for worse, for richer, for poorer, in sickness and in health." Through prosperity and adversity the two are partners, supporting each other and sharing alike in the good times and in the bad.

The third clause of the marriage vow calls for the two to become "one flesh" (*basar;* Genesis 2:24). This signifies a growing together. As two trees planted close to each other may eventually merge so that for all practical purposes they have one trunk, so two individuals may, through long association, find their purposes and values to have merged into a set of shared goals. Yet just as the two plants will each continue to produce its own flowers, so the marriage partners are to maintain their individuality. Each person is accountable to God individually, not through another person—not even through a spouse.

The joining together of the marriage partners finds its physical expression in their children, the product of their sexual union. God's plan was that the partners would "be fruitful and multiply; fill the earth" and produce "godly offspring" (Genesis 1:28; Malachi 2:15). Children not only are physical expressions of their parents' becoming one flesh, but they naturally give the parents a common interest and responsibility. The marriage covenant extends to the care and nurture of the children (Ephesians 6:4) and the transmission of the image of God to the next generation.

In the Bible, *covenant* is a serious word, and the marriage covenant is no exception. Those who violate the marriage covenant are compared to traitors.[5] Adultery is such a serious crime that the prohibition against it is one of the Ten Commandments (Exodus 20:14). The New Testament repeats this prohibition (Acts 15:20), and it warns that unrepentant adulterers will be excluded from heaven (Galatians 5:19–21; Revelation 21:8). The seriousness of breaking the marriage covenant is highlighted by the biblical comparison of marriage to God's relationship with His people.

The spiritual meaning of marriage

The drive to form social relationships is part of the image of God. We can see it in the mysterious union of the Trinity and as it is reflected in both the male and the female. So, the marriage relationship is a metaphor explicating the relationship of God and His people. God repeatedly compares His relationship with His people to a marriage (Isaiah 62:5; Jeremiah 31; Hosea 2:19, 20; Matthew 9:15; 25:1–13). He says, "Your Maker is your husband" (Isaiah 54:5), and He frequently compares unfaithfulness in worship to unfaithfulness in marriage (Numbers 25:1; Ezekiel 20:30–32; Hosea 4:17–19).

There is a correlation between the three clauses of the wedding covenant and the relationship between God and His people. As the marriage partners are to leave all else, so God's people must leave all other relationships that threaten to take the place of their relationship to Him (Exodus 20:3–6). This includes relationships with "father and mother" (Matthew 10:37) and much more. God calls us to value our relationship with Him above everything else, whether work, play, hobbies, wealth, entertainment, or intellect. When Jesus called Matthew, he "left all, rose up, and followed Him" (Luke 5:28).

We also see the similarity of the relationship between God and the believer to that of marriage in the "joining together." As the husband and wife are to cling to each other, so we must hold fast to God. It is not enough for us to abstain from sin; we must also practice the good— we must seek to live in such a way as to be a positive blessing to others. And we must spend time in prayer and Bible study. Jesus said, "Abide in Me, and I in you" (John 15:4). This "abiding" requires a steadfast "clinging" to God and a refusal to allow anything to separate us from Him. As God's people spend time with Him, they are changed into His likeness (2 Corinthians 3:18). Jesus said, "I am the vine, you are the branches. He who abides in Me, and I in him, bears much fruit; for without Me you can do nothing" (John 15: 5). In the marriage relationship, abiding in each other brings growth, and abiding in Christ brings spiritual growth.

Because the relationship between the Creator God and His people is likened to a marriage, unfaithfulness to that relationship amounts to spiritual adultery. The Creator God is the "husband" of His people (Isaiah 54:5). To exalt a theory that replaces Him as Creator is to cling to someone or something other than our spiritual "husband"—a form of spiritual adultery. Just before the end of the world, the three angels' messages of Revelation 14 call all people everywhere to faithful worship (Revelation 14:6–12). The first angel calls upon humans to worship the Creator and to prepare for judgment. Those who reject this message receive the second message—the warning against spiritual adultery, against turning away from their spiritual Spouse, the Creator, to another creator, the false one put forward by the theory of evolution. Rather than worshiping the Creator, those who turn to the substitute spouse worship the creature, believing that the powers of creation lie within nature itself (Romans 1:22–25). This is spiritual adultery, and it will end in the destruction described in the message of the third angel. The vivid imagery of the three angels' messages uses marital infidelity to emphasize the seriousness with which God, as Creator and Judge, regards His relationship to the church.

Creation and marriage

The Creation story provides the basis for the marriage covenant as it was divinely instituted. Evolutionary theory provides a totally different standard for sexual behavior. This can be illustrated by considering three aspects of marriage: permanence, sexual fidelity, and the value of children. The implications of creation for each of these stands in strong contrast to the implications of evolutionary theory.

Permanence. The commitment made in a biblical marriage is a permanent one, lasting as long as both partners remain alive. Jesus made this point when He responded to the question of divorce by stating that no human is to separate "what God has joined together" (Mark 10:9). He said God permitted divorce only because of the hardness of human hearts (verse 5). Paul also affirmed the principle that married couples should stay together (1 Corinthians 7:10, 11). It may be better to separate than to stay in a relationship in which there is infidelity (Matthew 19:9) or violence (1 Corinthians 7:15), but this is a result of human sinfulness, not a part of the original plan for marriage.

In contrast, evolutionary theory provides no principles that call for maintaining permanence in marriage. In evolutionary theory, the goal of relationships that involve sexual intercourse is to pass on the maximum number of one's genes to the next generation. The sexual partner is valued primarily for the help he or she can provide in passing along one's genes. If a partner can't help with this, the principles on which evolution operates say one should get a different partner. In some species, pairs may remain together while they're raising their young, but not necessarily permanently. In many species, there is no pair bonding, and mating is opportunistic.

The biblical story of Creation shows that the permanence of marriage is a moral issue. Evolution pictures mating as merely a means of passing along one's genes.

Sexual fidelity. In marriage, sexual fidelity to one's marriage partner is an important and highly valued biblical principle. The well-being of the entire family is enhanced by a stable and faithful relationship; the Bible condemns adultery in the strongest possible terms (see Exodus 20:14; 1 Corinthians 6:9, 10). In contrast, evolutionary theory holds that sexual fidelity is generally disadvantageous. If humans evolved from animals, we wouldn't expect them to value or practice sexual fidelity. Animals vary in their mating systems, and evolution expects humans to do the same.

Three major mating systems have been found among animals. Some animals, such as many species of deer and antelope, are polygamous. A single male collects a harem of females, and that male sires nearly all of the offspring.

Apparent monogamy is another mating system found among animals. In this system, a single male mates with a single female. Many birds and mammals mate in this way—especially those in which both parents care for the offspring. However, genetic fingerprinting has revealed that some of the offspring of these creatures have fathers other than the ones in the original pair. In other words, the female has mated with more than one male, and her offspring have multiple fathers. So, they aren't truly monogamous after all—they only appear to be monogamous.

The third type of mating system is promiscuity, in which any male can mate with any female. This system is common among animals, especially in those species in which the male doesn't help care for the offspring.

If God chose to bring the human lineage into existence through evolutionary creation, we would expect Him to approve of them following one or more of these mating systems. But He doesn't approve of these systems. Thus Creation, not evolution, is the basis for sexual morality.

The value of offspring. In the Creation story, the very first command given to humans was to be fruitful and multiply (Genesis 1:28). After the Fall, God said that someone would destroy the serpent, and this Savior would come from the "Seed," or Offspring, of the woman (Genesis 3:15). Jesus declared that the kingdom of heaven would be made up of people who were like children (Matthew 19:14). And children, like adult humans, bear the image of God. From the perspective that the biblical story of Creation establishes, all of these factors give children value.

However, viewed from the perspective of evolution, the value of offspring is based on their carrying the genes of their parents. The more offspring that survive to reproduce, the more successfully are the genes of the parents transmitted. So, evolution views inferior offspring as burdens that are best eliminated. The logic of evolution suggests that if natural selection isn't working, we should consider using artificial selection, or eugenics, to improve the quality of the species. Evolutionary theory provides no basis for opposing such practices as infanticide and selective breeding.

Humans have always experienced problems in their relationships. Evolutionary theory is part of the largely subconscious cultural background that acts to reduce respect for the marriage covenant. No one can make a convincing case that evolutionary theory has strengthened the foundation of marriage! Instead, it is compatible with and even supports promiscuity, serial polygamy, sexual infidelity, and eugenics. The arguments of evolutionists who object to these practices on moral grounds rest on the foundation of creation whether or not they recognize this.

Morality in marriage is based on creation. It is logically inconsistent to reject the biblical account of the special creation of Adam and Eve and their joining in marriage by divine arrangement, while at the same time insisting on moral principles that ultimately are founded on creation. But it isn't unusual to see this happening. The practice of choosing philosophical elements from mutually contradictory worldviews has appropriately been called "philosophical cheating."[6]

Conclusion

Marriage is a gift that God gave to our first parents in Eden—a gift that is a great blessing and an evidence of God's love for humanity despite the fact that sin has damaged it. The biblical Creation story provides the logical foundation for marriage, and rejection of that story has weakened the institution. Evolutionary theory logically leads to a secular view of sexual behavior, which destroys the moral foundations of marriage and also its meaning for the relationship of humans with their Creator. Christian marriage is built on the values of permanence, sexual fidelity, and the value of all children, and, where faithfully practiced, contributes to the well-being of society.

---

1. See Davidson, R. *Flame of Yahweh: Sexuality in the Old Testament.* Peabody, MA: Hendrickson (2007), chapters 1, 2.

2. That is the meaning of the Hebrew word used here, *banah* (Genesis 2:22).

3. Note that Hebrew poetry involves "thought rhyme," or repetition of an idea.

4. Possibly excepting Genesis 2:2, 3; see Moskala, J. "A Fresh Look at Two Genesis Creation Accounts: Contradictions?" *Andrews University Seminary Studies* 49/1(2011):56.

5. Collins, CJ. (2006), 143; commenting on Proverbs 23:27, 28; cf. Malachi 2:14–16.

6. Pearcey, NR. *Total Truth: Liberating Christianity From Its Cultural Captivity.* Wheaton, IL: Crossway Books (2005), 319–321.

CHAPTER 10

Creation and Environmental Care

Every thoughtful person recognizes the importance of caring for our environment. We depend on it for our food, air, and water, and for materials for clothing, shelter, transportation, and communication. The Bible identifies God as the ultimate Provider of all these things, and the Creation story records our appointment as stewards to care for them. As stewards, we are caretakers on behalf of the Creator. It would be foolish for us to be careless in managing our responsibilities, and it would be equally foolish to regard the gifts as greater than the Giver. Christians have at times been guilty of both errors. At the present time, the health of our environment is under threat, and it is imperative that we develop a biblically based response to the things that threaten the health of our environment.

Humankind's responsibilities to the environment are first identified in the Creation story. When God created Adam and Eve, He gave them a threefold assignment in the form of a blessing (Genesis 1:28). Each of the three parts of this assignment has implications for the environment.

First, God told Adam and Eve that they were to "fill[1] the earth." God repeated this part of the assignment to Noah after the Flood (Genesis 9:1), even though the land had been cursed and the earth's surface disrupted. God may not be asking us today to do the same—there's a limit to the number of people the earth can support, and we seem to be close to that limit, though there probably are enough resources to support the global population if those resources are freely and equitably distributed.

Second, Adam and Eve were to "subdue" (*kabash*) the earth. The Hebrew word means literally "to bring under control," as when a king "subdues" his domain (cf. 1 Chronicles 22:18). This requires careful arrangement of houses, farms, and wild lands, and proper management of soil and water. Done right, the result would be a peaceful and productive land.

Third, the human pair were told to hold dominion (*radah*) over the other creatures that live on the earth—whether in the sea, in the air, or on the land. The idea here is of rulership. Good rulers keep the best interests of those they govern in mind, while bad rulers govern for their own benefit. God rules for the benefit of His creatures; we who are appointed as His stewards should do the same.

Genesis 2 identifies some other aspects of the role God assigned to humans. In the beginning, He gave Adam the task of naming the animals. Adam "called" (*qara;* Genesis 2:19) the animals by name. This parallels what God did in naming day and night, heaven, earth, and sea (Genesis 1:5, 8, 10). This indicates that God gave Adam dominion over the animals, but not over the physical environment.

When God placed Adam in the Garden of Eden, He used two other terms in laying out his tasks. Adam was to "tend"; literally, to "serve" (*ʿabad*) the Garden (Genesis 2:15). Adam's service to the Garden would include the work of tending the plants and keeping them under control. In return, the Garden would "serve" Adam by providing food for him.

God also told Adam that he was to "keep" or to "guard" (*shamar*) the Garden. The same word is used of the task God assigned the cherubim to carry out after Adam and Eve sinned: the cherubim were to "guard" the way to the tree of life (Genesis 3:24). This implies that Adam's rule was to be benevolent. He was to guard the Garden and, by implication, the entire world, against the intrusion of any bad thing. Sadly, Adam failed this assignment: he allowed the devil access to the world—which, as we know, resulted in great harm both to the earth's environment and to the creatures living here.

A steward is someone appointed to carry out a responsibility on behalf of the owner of some piece of property. To be a good steward, a person needs to be able to manage the property in the way the owner wishes. As the owner of the earth, God appointed Adam and his descendants to be His stewards, and He equipped them for the task by endowing them with His image. This included the skills needed to provide responsible and benevolent rule, to cultivate healthy relationships, and to exercise appropriate moral judgment. Humankind's dominion requires a clear mind, a healthy body, and a benevolent attitude toward the governed. These attributes are part of the image of God expressed in humans.

A good steward will seek to understand the will of the owner and will exert every effort to fulfill the owner's wishes. What is God's will for the creation? Obviously, God wills for it to exist because He created it (Revelation 4:11). As good stewards, we will cooperate in maintaining the existence of what God has created.

God has stated the reason He created the earth: He "formed it to be inhabited" (Isaiah 45:18). Because God intentionally created the earth with the purpose that human beings should exist for His glory (Isaiah 43:7), His stewards would be violating His will if they were to destroy the creation that He meant to provide the things that people need. The heavenly beings affirm this, calling on God to bring an end to sin and to "destroy those who destroy the earth" (Revelation 11:18). These texts should guide our thinking as we develop principles of good stewardship.

Stewardship and care for the other creatures

God cares about His creatures, and as His stewards, so should we. Genesis describes the creation of diverse kinds of creatures in terms that show that God wanted them to fill the land and the sea (Genesis 1:22, 28). God shows His continuing interest in the well-being of the animals by providing what they must have if they are to survive (Psalm 104). After creating the animals of the sky and sea, God looked them over and declared them "good." Again, after creating the land animals, God called them "good." Because God considers it good that the earth be filled with diverse creatures, we should also consider their existence good, even though they now live in a fallen world.

God cares about the animals even in their fallen state. When He told Noah to build an ark, He told him to build it large enough to save the animals as well as the people, indicating that He wanted them to survive the catastrophe (Genesis 6:19–7:3). And when the Flood was over, God "remembered"[2] not only Noah, but also "every living thing, and all the animals that were with him in the ark" (Genesis 8:1).

Note also that when God gave Israel the Sabbath commandment, He said the domestic animals were to rest on that day along with the people—He said the people were to work six days and rest the seventh "that your ox and your donkey may rest" (Exodus 23:10; see also 20:10). We see a similar concern for the animals in God's instructions concerning the sabbatical year. The Israelites were to leave the land fallow every seventh year and let the poor and the beasts of the field eat whatever they wanted to (Exodus 23:11; Leviticus 25:4–7).

The book of Job reveals that God takes joy in the creatures He has made. He challenged Job by pointing to His own knowledge of and care for His creatures, naming specific examples (Job 38:29–39:30). He spoke of the strength of the wild ox and the horse, the speed of the ostrich and the horse, and the flight of the hawk, and pointed out the provision of food for the lion and the raven, and of food and freedom for the wild donkey.

God then described in more detail two impressive creatures: the behemoth and the leviathan. He said, "Look now at the behemoth, *which I made along with you*" (Job 40:15; emphasis added). This seems intended to impress Job that just as God valued Adam and Eve, so He also values the behemoth and the other animals He created—that is not to say that He valued them the same; just that He valued them both.[3] The other creature God joyfully described for Job was the leviathan. Again, the identity is uncertain, but in this case the crocodile is the best candidate.[4]

Human stewardship includes care for the animals and concern for their well-being. This extends even to those creatures we may rightfully fear.

Probably the most significant threat to wildlife today is habitat destruction. As good stewards, we should seek ways to preserve the diversity of God's creatures by preserving appropriate habitats and ensuring that the necessities of life are available to the creatures that live there. This will sometimes mean we have to make difficult choices—for instance, whether to develop an area for human use or to preserve it for the benefit of wild animals. Too often, such decisions are made solely on financial grounds rather than on the basis of the actual needs of both humans and wildlife. Good stewardship isn't based on greed, but on thoughtful consideration of the needs of all parties affected.

While we must care for both domesticated and wild animals, we shouldn't do so at the expense of human life. Animals that kill humans are to be killed (Genesis 9:5, 6). Doing so reduces the threat to humans by preventing the development of man-eaters and helps reduce the likelihood of developing animals with a genetic tendency toward such behavior.

Sometimes we may have to reduce the numbers of animals in order to maintain the health of the population or to achieve a harmonious balance of nature. When this is necessary, it should be done as mercifully as possible.

Stewardship and care for the physical environment

The Creator has provided the physical environment needed to support life, and He is concerned with the way we care for the land, air, and water. He hasn't given us the power to control the sea, the atmosphere, or the continents, but we are able to corrupt the earth's surface by poor environmental practices, so we must not ignore our responsibility to maintain a healthy physical environment.

Hundreds of books and articles have been written on the topic of care for the physical environment, and the interested reader can easily find additional information. Here, we will briefly consider just two aspects of this topic: the effects of pollution and excessive consumption of earth's resources.

Pollution of the environment has reached such proportions that it is affecting the health of both humans and animals. Exhaust from cars, trucks, airplanes, and factories introduces noxious chemicals into the air. These chemical irritants and toxins can cause disease in the animals that breathe them, can impair the growth of plants, and can even kill people whose health is poor. The particles exhausted into the air will eventually settle out of it, but then can cause additional damage in the form of acid rain and acidified lakes that stunt the growth of fish and other aquatic organisms.

Another major source of pollution is solid waste from households and factories. For example, plastic bags and plastic bottles resist degradation for years and tend to accumulate in the environment. They can be washed into rivers and eventually into the oceans, where they accumulate. This problem has reached such proportions that someone has named a part of the North Pacific Ocean "the Great Pacific Garbage Patch."[5] An estimated one hundred million tons of waste float in the water there—pieces of plastic, chemical sludge, and miscellaneous kinds of trash. Both the plastics and the chemicals harm the wildlife that swallow them. No doubt the effects will become worse as more wastes are washed into the Pacific.

We can help care for our environment by limiting our consumption of natural resources and thereby reducing our demands on the physical environment. One simple way to do this is to recycle materials such as plastics, paper, and metals. Recycling gives the added benefit of reducing pollution—especially the accumulation of plastic products in the environment.

Another good habit is to live simply. If we purchase only the things we really need, and keep and use them as long as possible, we will help limit demands on the physical environment. Eating foods made from plants rather than those made from animals also helps. It takes much more water and energy to raise animals than it does to raise plants. (Plant-based diets benefit not only the environment, but also human health.)

Caring for the physical environment is part of our responsibility as stewards. The health and well-being of future generations, both of animals and humans, depends on the way we treat the environment now. This should motivate us to live simply and responsibly, managing carefully our consumption, our household waste, and other potential sources of pollution.

Stewardship and care for human well-being

Stewardship also involves caring for the health and well-being of humans. God's care for humans is expressed in many ways. He provides the necessities of life (Matthew 6:33).[6] He gives instructions on how to keep our bodies strong and healthy (e.g., Leviticus 11–15; see also Genesis 1:29; Leviticus 7:15–27; Numbers 19:11–22; Deuteronomy 23:12–14;

Acts 15:20). And He provides information that gives purpose for our lives and hope for the future (John 14:1–3; cf. Genesis 12:1–3; Isaiah 11; Daniel 2:44). As God's stewards, we have responsibilities—among them, cooperating with Him in all our activities.

We are called to cooperate with God in providing the necessities of life to those in need. Personal ministry is the most effective means of doing this. There are needy people—elderly widows, single-parent families, prisoners, or people with handicaps—within the reach of each of us. If we keep our eyes open, we'll find plenty of opportunities to help. We can help indirectly, too, by contributing money, time, and material to organizations that minister to the needy. In this way, the benefits of ministry can be multiplied.

Good stewards will cooperate with God in the care of their own bodies and by helping others understand the rules of good health. The citizens of the Western world, where much of the diet consists of "fast foods" rich in sugar and fat, particularly need to develop good dietary habits. Fast foods exacerbate the problem of diabetes, which in some areas now afflicts a majority of the population. Caring for others also means telling them about the benefits of exercise, fresh air, sunlight, pure water, proper rest, and so forth, and in some cases it means helping people obtain medical care.

Mental health is another vital aspect of human well-being that falls within the purview of good stewardship. We may cooperate with the Creator by sharing the hope He has given in His Word. Life may seem meaningless and death preferable to people who feel crushed by the burdens they're carrying and who have no hope for the future. God has made promises to us for the future. He's given us a reason to live and a basis for hope. Sin has damaged the beautiful world God created, but this world won't remain in its current condition forever. God has promised a bright future to everyone who trusts Him. Many would love to hear this good news. We can cooperate with the Creator by pointing them to the promises of God and showing in our own lives that we truly believe them ourselves.

Contributing to the health and well-being of humanity is an important part of the work of those who would be stewards for the Creator.

He calls us to minister to the sick, to relieve the suffering of the poor and disadvantaged, and to bid others to follow Him (Isaiah 58:6–12; Micah 6:8; Matthew 25:31–46; 28:18–20).

Conclusion

The biblical doctrine of Creation affects the way we pursue our roles as stewards. We seek to model our behavior on the example set by the Creator, who values all creatures, but humans most of all (Luke 12:7). The doctrine of Creation helps us maintain a balanced approach to stewardship. It says we should avoid the extreme of showing callous disregard for the environment, treating it as nothing more than a money pit open to our greed and exploitation, and we should also avoid the other extreme of regarding nature as divine and worthy of worship, and considering the animals to have the same value as do the people.

This physical world has great value because it was made by the God who made us and who loves His creation. It is intended for our benefit, and we, in turn, have been appointed to care for it. That is what it means to be a good steward.

---

1. Hebrew *male'*, to fill, replenish, satisfy.

2. Hebrew *zakar*. The same word is used in Genesis 19:29, which says God "remembered" Abraham and saved Lot from the destruction of Sodom; and in Exodus 2:24, which says God "remembered" His covenant with Abraham, Isaac, and Jacob, and prepared to deliver the Israelites from Egyptian bondage.

3. Just what animal the behemoth was is not certain, but the hippopotamus is a likely candidate. Both the behemoth and the hippo feed on grass, are large and strong, live near water, and don't mind the swiftness of the river. Some have objected on the basis that the hippo has a small tail, not one like a cedar, which is a tree. But the text doesn't say the tail is like a cedar. It says the behemoth *moves* his tail like a cedar (Job 40:17). There is no basis for supposing the behemoth was some kind of dinosaur. Fossil hippopotamuses have been found in the Jordan Valley. Tchernov, E. "The Paleobiogeographical History of the Southern Levant," in Y. Yom-Tov and E. Tchernov, eds. *The Zoogeography of Israel*. Boston: Dr. W. Junk Publishers (1988), 213.

4. Both the crocodile and the leviathan live in water, have impressive teeth and scales, are fearless, and are too strong and fierce for humans to fight (Job 41:1–34). No doubt we should consider the statement that fire and smoke shoot out of his nostrils to be metaphorical, and again, there is no basis for thinking the description here could be a reference to a dinosaur. Crocodiles were native to Israel until the last one was shot in the early 1900s. Ibid., 230.

5. See http://en.wikipedia.org/wiki/Great_Pacific_Ocean_Garbage_Patch. Other oceans also have "garbage patches."

6. Seen in the provisions of Creation week.

CHAPTER 11

Creation and the Sabbath

The richness of the meaning of the seventh-day Sabbath is seldom appreciated as it could be. The observance of the seventh-day Sabbath is a witness to our faith in the biblical account of a six-day Creation and seventh-day rest and all that this means. And it means a lot. The Creation story reveals much about God, about our world, and about us—all of which is symbolized by the biblical Sabbath. In this chapter, we will explore some of the meaning inherent in the seventh-day Sabbath. We will begin by reviewing two scripture passages that deal with the Sabbath.

Genesis 2:1–3 presents the basis for the seventh-day Sabbath. The text reads: "Thus the heavens and the earth were finished, and all the host of them. And on the seventh day God ended his work which he had made; and he rested on the seventh day from all his work which he had made. And God blessed the seventh day, and sanctified it: because that in it he had rested from all his work which God created and made" (KJV).

This passage makes several important points.

A completed work. At the end of the first six days, the work of creation was completed (*kalah;* Genesis 2:1, 2). God had filled the heavens and the earth, and they were functioning as He intended. Nothing else was needed.

What God felt when He finished His work of creation must have been similar to what we feel when we finish constructing a building. The Hebrew word translated "completed" in this passage is the same as the word used when Solomon's temple was "*finished* in all its details and according to all its plans" (1 Kings 6:38; emphasis added).

The seventh day. God rested on the seventh day of that first week. We can infer two points from this statement. First, six days had to pass before God rested in order for the day of rest to be called the seventh day. There could be no seventh day on which to observe the Sabbath rest without the preceding six days of Creation week. The numbering of the days of the week is patterned after the six days of Creation, and the identity of the seventh day is rooted in the Creation week.

Second, the seventh day is a literal day. The seventh-day Sabbath has always been observed as a literal day of twenty-four hours.[1]

The description of the seventh day is the only description of a day of Creation week that doesn't end with the mention of an "evening" and a "morning." God's activity on the seventh day differed from His activity on the preceding days. On each of the six days of Creation, God had completed that day's work by the end of the day. In contrast, God's rest from creating didn't end when the seventh day ended, but continues to our day and beyond. In referring to the creation, the writer of Hebrews says, "The works were finished from the foundation of the world" (Hebrews 4:3). At some point in the future, God will create again (2 Peter 3:13). Presently, His work in this world isn't that of creating but of sustaining.

God rested. When the creation was completed, God rested from creating. Literally, He "sabbathed" (*shabat*) from His work. The word carries the meaning of stopping what one was doing because the project is finished, not because one is tired. When attorneys "rest" their case, they stop presenting it—not because they're tired of speaking but because they've completed their presentation; they've said all they want to say. Similarly, God rested because He had completed what He had set out to do. "He rested from all his work which God had created and made" (Genesis 2:3).[2] This doesn't mean that God had nothing further to do with what He had created. Far from it. God continues to maintain and govern creation.[3] He has ceased "creating" and "making" because He has completed the project.

God blessed the seventh day. This is the third blessing God gave at Creation. On days five and six, He blessed the creatures He had made. He directed the Sabbath blessing to a period of time—the Sabbath day. The first two blessings were for fertility and filling the earth. Can the Sabbath blessing mean any less? The Sabbath blessing is an assurance that God will provide all that is needed.

God sanctified it. The word *sanctify* means "to dedicate as holy." The seventh day was the very first thing to be identified as holy. Later, places were declared to be holy—the ground around the burning bush, the Holy Place of the tabernacle, the city of Jerusalem, and so on. God also instructed that other things—and people—were to be sanctified or made holy: among them, the sacrifices, the priests, and the people of God. All of these have in common God's intention that His presence be manifest. When God sanctified the Sabbath, He meant that it should be reserved for His presence.

The Sabbath commandment

The second Sabbath passage is the Sabbath commandment as recorded in Exodus 20:8–11. God Himself spoke this commandment in His own words as He had the others. He said, "Remember the sabbath day, to keep it holy. Six days shalt thou labour, and do all thy work: but the seventh day is the sabbath of the Lord thy God: in it thou shalt not do any work. . . . For in six days the Lord made heaven and earth, the sea, and all that in them is, and rested the seventh day: wherefore the Lord blessed the sabbath day, and hallowed it" (KJV).

This text uses language strikingly similar to that used in the description of the seventh day of Creation week. Important parallels in wording include "day," "holy" ("sanctified"), "work," "heaven," "earth," "rested," "blessed," and "sanctified." The language emphatically points back to the Creation week described in Genesis.

Remember the Sabbath. The Sabbath wasn't something new—an addition to the worship activities of God's people. No, it had existed since Creation, as the language of the text reveals. The problem was that it had been forgotten by a people in slavery. The Ten Commandments brought it to mind again.

The Sabbath wasn't created in response to the arrival of sin. It hearkens back to the seventh day of Creation week, before sin came into the world. Nor was the Sabbath a politically motivated institution, one meant to give identity to a new nation. It is a blessing intended for all people. As all humans have descended from the pair created in Eden, so all humans are to enjoy the blessings of the Sabbath that God gave in that place and time. This is part of what it means to remember the Sabbath.

Remembering the Sabbath also means remembering its past and remembering what God has told us about what it will be in the future. The past dimension of the Sabbath is its role of reminding us that God created our race, and He invested us with individuality and gave us the privilege of bearing His image. It includes also the closeness to God we experience as we remember the Sabbath blessings we have had. As for the future, each week we are to remember to prepare both for the coming Sabbath and for the "rest that remains"—the rest we will know in the kingdom of God (Hebrews 4:9; Isaiah 65:22, 23).

Linguistic parallels with Genesis 2:1–3. As noted above, several of the key words in the Sabbath commandment were also used in the description in Genesis 2:1–3 of God's rest from His work of creating. The first of these is "day" (*yom*). The Sabbath day in both the commandment and the Creation account is a specific, literal day.

Another key word is "holy" (*qadesh*). The Sabbath day is to be kept "holy" because at the end of Creation week God "hallowed" it and "sanctified" it. The same Hebrew word is used in all three cases.

The phrase "Sabbath [*shabbath*] of the Lord" (Exodus 20:10) refers back to Genesis 2:2, 3, which says God rested (*shabat*) on the seventh day. The Hebrew words are nearly identical. The seventh-day Sabbath is a memorial of God's rest after His "work" (*mela'kah;* Genesis 2:3) of completing the creation of the heavens (*shamayim*) and earth (*'eretz*) in six literal days. Likewise, we are to rest from our work on the seventh day. This doesn't mean we should refrain from all activity. As on the Sabbath day God continues to sustain what He created, so we should continue to sustain life on that day.

A seventh significant word common to the two passages is "blessed" (*barak*).[4] Both Genesis 2:3 and Exodus 20:11 say that God blessed the seventh day. In both passages the blessing is linked with the day's having been "hallowed" or "sanctified" (*qadesh*), which is another close parallel the passages contain. The similarities in the language of the two passages show the strong link between the seventh-day Sabbath and Creation week.

Why we keep the Sabbath

There are two aspects to the question of why we keep the seventh-day Sabbath. The first is the narrower, more specific matter of the seventh day: why do we keep the Sabbath on the seventh day? The answer to that question is that we pattern what we do upon what God did, and He worked six days and rested on the seventh day. The second aspect is the broader question of why we observe Sabbath at all.

One reason for Sabbath keeping is given in Deuteronomy 5. In this book, the farewell address Moses gave just before his death, he reviews the Israelites' history and lays out for them how they should conduct their lives. Among his other instructions, he says they should observe "the Sabbath [rest] of the Lord your God" (Deuteronomy 5:12–15). The "rest" of God obviously refers to His "rest" after the six days of Creation, but Moses provides another reason for keeping the Sabbath commandment: it was this Creator God who delivered them from slavery. Because of this, they should obey Him rather than any other god. In verse 6, this same point was applied to all of the Ten Commandments, which are restated here.

A second reason for observing the Sabbath is emphatically given in Exodus 31:12–17. Here, God tells the Israelites that they should "keep" (*shamar*) the Sabbath—God's rest. The word translated "keep" here is the same word that was used to describe Adam's job—he was to "keep" the Garden—and also for the work of the angels stationed at the entrance to the Garden; they were to "keep," in other words, to guard, the tree of life (Genesis 3:24). Thus, to "keep" the Sabbath is to guard its holiness.

According to this passage, the Sabbath is a sign that God is "the Lord who sanctifies you" (verse 13; cf. Ezekiel 20:12). As God set the seventh day apart and blessed and sanctified it at the close of Creation week, so He sanctifies us—sets us apart—for special blessing. Observance of the seventh-day Sabbath is a public recognition that we are fallen creatures. We were created morally better than we are now, and we are completely dependent on God's creative power for our salvation. Sabbath is a sign or recognition of God's covenantal promise that He will sanctify His people.

The Sabbath symbolizes all these points, but only the six-day Creation explains why the Sabbath is the seventh day of the week rather than some other day. It may be tempting to wonder if one could ignore the Creation story and justify Sabbath keeping solely on the basis of the deliverance from Egypt, but such thinking applies the Sabbath only to the Jews. The link between the seventh-day Sabbath and the six days of Creation reminds us that the seventh-day Sabbath was meant for all people.

The symbolic meaning of the Sabbath

The Sabbath has a depth of meaning that offers many blessings to those who study it. We'll briefly review some of the rich meaning it contains.[5]

Sabbath and God. The Sabbath reminds us of the Creator God and His desire to bless our lives with His presence. The very first full day of human existence was a Sabbath; it was a time of fellowship between God and the first humans. With the entrance of sin, the Sabbath added meaning as it became a reminder of God's plan to restore us to fellowship with Him.

The Sabbath is a reminder of the generosity of God. At the end of the six days of Creation, the world was complete. God had already provided everything that the beings He had created would need. The Sabbath is a symbol of His generosity, and it reminds us that He has provided not only for our physical needs, but also for our spiritual needs. It is a promise that we don't have to earn our salvation; we can rest in what God has provided.

Creation and the Sabbath

Sabbath and the world. The Sabbath is a reminder of God's ongoing care for the world. As God worked during Creation week to originate the world, He works now to sustain it. When God was creating the world, He established the seasons (Genesis 1:14). Now He sends the sun and the rain. When God was creating, He made the necessities of life. Now He sustains life from day to day (Psalm 103:2–5; Acts 17:25).

Sabbath is also a reminder of God's promise to restore the world to its original goodness. Sin brought a series of curses on the world, resulting in degeneration, suffering, and death. To some extent, the Flood reversed the events of Creation.[6] In keeping the Sabbath, we work with God to hasten the day of restoration. Sabbath is a promise of restoration—a promise that eventually God will return the world to harmony with Him, that He will bring about a new creation.

Sabbath and humankind. Sabbath is a reminder that we were endowed with the image of God. As God rested that first week, so those made in His image are to rest on the seventh day of each week. We may doubt ourselves at times, but the Sabbath reminds us that God values us enough to entrust us with His image.

The Sabbath is a reminder of God's intention to bring us back to fellowship with Him. It reminds us not only of our fallenness, but also of God's promise to restore His image in us and to restore peaceful relationships among humans. Sabbath reminds us also of the creative power needed to sanctify sinners. Our faith in His saving grace is not mere presumption, but rests on the facts of the Creation week, during which God's word gave existence and form to the objects He created. The original goodness of the creation during that first Sabbath is an assurance of the goodness of God's character and the reliability of His promises of salvation.

Jesus and the Sabbath

Jesus showed us God's intention for the Sabbath. He attended synagogue on the Sabbath—He was found in the house of worship on that day (Luke 4:16–20). Sabbath is dedicated or set apart for sacred purposes. Public worship is one such purpose, and Jesus participated in public worship. But Jesus didn't do all His teaching in public meetings;

He also taught while walking in the fields (Luke 6:1–5) and while eating in homes (Luke 14:1–6). Worship is an integral part of the Sabbath.

Jesus also gave us an example of Sabbath keeping in what He did to relieve suffering (e.g., Luke 6:6–11). When the work of creation ended, the work of sustaining began, and healing the sick is part of the work of sustaining the creation. That work that began on the first Sabbath continues today. It is appropriate for us to bring relief on the Sabbath to those who are suffering.

Worship of God involves both spirit and truth (John 4:24). Neither can be ignored. Jesus showed us how to worship in truth with His teaching and participation in public worship. He showed us how to worship in spirit with His healing and His ministry to the suffering. His followers can do no better than to follow His example.

Creation and Sabbath keeping

The practice of keeping the seventh-day Sabbath is unavoidably linked with a literal six-day Creation. First, the numbering of the days is based on the Creation week. The seventh day on which God rested is explicitly identified as the one that came immediately after the six days of Creation.

Second, the phrase "God's Sabbath" is based on the Creation week. God's "Sabbath" is God's "rest," and the idea that God rested has no meaning apart from the work of creation. If God didn't spend six days in creating, what would be the meaning of His spending the seventh day resting? The very term "sabbath" implies a rest from creating and derives its significance from the Creation story in Genesis.

A third way in which a six-day Creation makes a difference for the Sabbath is in the scope of the Sabbath. The Bible describes the creation of the ancestors of all humans on the sixth day of Creation week. The commandment that mandates Sabbath observance on the seventh day of the week uses the same definitive words that are used in the record of God's activities on the seventh day of Creation week, showing that the Sabbath applies to all of humanity. If one rejects the six-day Creation, one removes the basis for universal Sabbath keeping, leaving the Sabbath an institution for the Jews that has but little relevance for Gentiles.

Conclusion

Observance of the seventh-day Sabbath is an expression of faith in the Creator God,

> who created a completed world in six days;
> who made all things very good, even giving the people He created free will, which they misused, corrupting the creation;
> and who promises to restore all that was lost.

Jesus, the Creator, came and showed us how to keep the Sabbath in spirit and in truth. The universality of the six-day Creation is the guarantee of the universality of the seventh-day Sabbath and the promise of universal restoration.

---

1. Exodus 16:23–26; cf. Luke 4:16. In the context of Creation, the Hebrew *yom* ("day") clearly means a literal day, as it is composed of an evening and a morning, is in a numbered sequence of days, and is commemorated by observance of a literal day.

2. Hebrew, *bara'* ("create") and *'asah* ("make"). These are the same two words used of God's creative activity during the six days of Creation.

3. See chapter 8 of this book.

4. The same word as in Genesis 2:2, 3.

5. For an excellent in-depth analysis of Sabbath meaning, see Tonstad, S. *The Lost Meaning of the Seventh Day.* Berrien Springs, MI: Andrews University Press (2009).

6. See Davidson, RM. "Biblical Evidence for the Universality of the Genesis Flood," in Baldwin, JT, ed. *Creation, Catastrophe, and Calvary.* Hagerstown, MD: Review and Herald® (2000), 79–92, references 17–25.

CHAPTER 12

The Good News of Creation

Adam's sin brought separation from God, but there's good news—God has provided a way for us to be restored to fellowship with Him. God sent His Son into the world to die in our place in order that we might share in His life. This simple message of the gospel is a golden thread that binds all Scripture into a promise of hope and restoration. The biblical teaching of Creation is intimately related to the gospel.

The first hint of the gospel was given by the Creator Himself in Eden to the only two humans in existence at the time. Adam and Eve had knowingly and willingly disobeyed the clear instructions of their Creator and had eaten the forbidden fruit. God called them to trial, where they reluctantly confessed. Next would be the sentencing. The serpent, which had brought the temptation, was sentenced first. Surprisingly, God chose to give the first hint of the good news in what He said to the serpent—before the fallen couple heard their punishment. God said, "I will put enmity between you [the serpent] and the woman, and between your seed and her Seed; He shall bruise your head, and you shall bruise His heel" (Genesis 3:15).

Three elements in this statement fill it with hope. First, God will put enmity (*'eybah*, hatred) between the serpent and the woman. Although the serpent had deceived the woman and caused her to break her relationship with her Creator, God would protect her from complete domination by the enemy. She had fallen into sin, but her freedom of choice was not lost. She would retain the ability to choose whether she would follow God or the deceiver.

Second, the woman would have a "seed" (*zera'*); in other words a child. This meant she wouldn't die immediately. Although her eventual death was certain, she would have the opportunity to raise a family and repent of her sin. It also meant that there would be a continuing conflict between her spiritual descendants and those of the enemy, culminating in the personal combat between Satan and her Seed, Jesus.[1]

Third, her Offspring would bruise (*shuph*, also "to crush") the head of the serpent-enemy, albeit at the cost of bruising His own heel. The serpent would eventually be destroyed, but at a cost. When God covered Adam and Eve with clothing made of animal skins (Genesis 3:21), they began to understand that the cost of their salvation would be very high. The story of Adam and Eve in the Garden is a story of grace. Salvation is a gift, and it comes at God's initiative, not our own.

The contrasting sacrifices of Abel and Cain indicate that at least some of those living at that time understood the deep meaning of the sacrifice. Abel brought a lamb from his flock, implying acceptance of his need for a savior and dependence on God. Cain, in contrast, ignored the Lord's provision and brought a sacrifice of his own choice, representing his attempt to win God's approval through his own efforts. Cain's offering of his own labor couldn't reconcile him to God, and it can't do so for us either. His acceptance of us is entirely a matter of grace.

Creation and the gospel in the life and death of Jesus

The life and ministry of Jesus reveal the relationship between Creation and the gospel in a number of ways. First, Christ is called the Second Adam, a clear reference to the Creation account in Genesis. Second, Christ's victory over the devil is spoken of (or written of) in terms derived from Genesis. Third, resurrection is a matter of creation comparable to the creation of Adam from the dust.

Christ the Second Adam. The correspondence between Christ and Adam is an important affirmation of the importance of Creation in the gospel story. Adam was the first human, whose sin brought death upon all his descendants. Christ came as the Second Adam (1 Corinthians 15:45) to bring life where Adam had brought death. Jesus said, "I have come that they may have life, and that they may have it more abundantly" (John 10:10). Although some may question the reality of Adam and Eve, the life and sacrifice of Jesus validate the Genesis story of these progenitors of the whole human race. They were real people, who really sinned, and who thus brought real physical death into the world.

Paul, however, writes of the hope Christ brought: "Now Christ is risen from the dead, and has become the firstfruits of those who have fallen asleep. For since by man came death, by Man also came the resurrection of the dead. For as in Adam all die, even so in Christ all shall be made alive" (1 Corinthians 15:20–22). Creation and the gospel are linked in the correspondence between the first Adam and Christ, the Second Adam.

The bruising of the serpent. The link between Creation and the gospel is also seen in certain references to the conflict between Christ and Satan. These references have their roots in the Genesis story of Creation and the Fall. For example, Paul refers to the "crushing" or "bruising" of Satan: "The God of peace will crush Satan under your feet shortly" (Romans 16:20). This is an echo of the promise given to Adam and Eve that the "Seed" of the woman would defeat the serpent. At the Cross, Satan's head was "bruised." He was defeated and will eventually be destroyed.[2] However, he's alive now and is still a force to be reckoned with.

Isaiah refers to bruising—in this case, the bruising of the Seed: "He was wounded for our transgressions, He was bruised [*daka'*] for our iniquities" (Isaiah 53:5). The Hebrew word for "bruised" here is different from the word translated "bruised" in Genesis 3, but the meanings are equivalent. Christ was literally bruised—He was beaten repeatedly (Matthew 27:26–31; Luke 22:63). But though He was beaten and bruised, He wasn't crushed or defeated. He gained the victory through His sufferings, and He won on our behalf too, because "by His stripes we are healed" (Isaiah 53:5).

Hebrews 2:14, 15 supplies us with another link to Genesis 3:15. Paul writes that "through death," Jesus would "destroy him who had the power of death, that is, the devil, and release those who through fear of death were all their lifetime subject to bondage."

Sin brought death (Genesis 3:19; Romans 5:12ff.), and the devil brought sin. The relationship between the devil and Christ, the "Seed" of the woman, is one of enmity, or hatred. There is an ongoing conflict between the two that results in both being "bruised," but Christ is clearly the Victor. As a result, both death and the devil will be destroyed (1 Corinthians 15:6; John 20:26–28). So, at the scene of the first sin, we hear the first promise of the gospel.

The Resurrection. A third link between Creation and the gospel is the creative power obvious in the Resurrection. Jesus rose from death through His own power: "My Father loves Me, because I lay down My life that I may take it again. No one takes it from Me, but I lay it down of Myself. I have power to lay it down, and I have power to take it again" (John 10:17, 18).

Life comes from Jesus, who is the Creator God. Jesus made several statements that indicate He is the Source of life. He made perhaps the clearest and strongest at the tomb of Lazarus. "I am the resurrection and the life," He said (John 11:25). On other occasions, He also said, "I am the way, the truth and the life" (John 14:6); "I am the bread of life" (John 6:48); and "I have come that they may have life" (John 10:10).

The bodily resurrection of Jesus was a real event in history. The risen Lord was seen by hundreds of people (John 20:26–28; 1 Corinthians 15:6). It was the reality of the Resurrection that gave power and boldness to the apostles (Acts 2:22–36). Jesus was a real human, with a real body, who really died and was resurrected bodily. More than any other single fact of history, it is the reality of the Resurrection that gives life to the Christian religion.

Resurrection from the dead is an act of creation similar to the creative acts that took place during Creation week, especially to the creation of Adam. God formed Adam from dust and then gave him life through His creative power. In similar fashion, through His own power, the Creator raised the lifeless body of Lazarus in what was an act of creation. That same power will again be exercised in the resurrection of the dead at the end of time (1 Corinthians 15:51, 52).[3] As Adam was formed from the dust, so the dead will be re-formed from the dust in the final resurrection. The creation of Adam from the dust gives us confidence that the same Creator God can re-create others who have died.

The resurrections of Jesus and of Lazarus also give us confidence that the persons resurrected at the end of the world will be the same persons who previously lived and died. The neural connections in the brain are destroyed by death, but God doesn't forget them. Jesus' disciples recognized Him after His resurrection (John 21:12); Lazarus's friends recognized him after his resurrection; and those who know us will recognize us after our resurrection (Job 19:25–27; 1 Corinthians 13:12). The God who created Adam's mind is able to re-create the minds of the rest of the dead.

Creation and the gospel at the time of the end

The relationship between Creation and the gospel is an important theme of the book of Revelation. The high point of the book may be the messages of the three angels depicted in Revelation 14:6–12.[4] Of special interest here is the first angel's message: "I saw another angel flying in the midst of heaven, having the everlasting gospel to preach to those who dwell on the earth—to every nation, tribe, tongue, and people— saying with a loud voice, 'Fear God and give glory to Him, for the hour of His judgment has come; and worship Him who made heaven and earth, the sea and springs of water' " (verses 6, 7).

Notice that Revelation says this angel has the gospel. Why then does he speak of judgment and Creation? Could the gospel be the message of judgment and Creation? We shall explore how these ideas are linked together.

The first angel's message links the gospel with the judgment and the Creation in a kind of parallelism:

a Fear God because of judgment.
a' Worship Him because of Creation.

There's a clear parallel between fearing God and worshiping Him. What then is the relationship between judgment and the gospel, and how do these relate to Creation?

Judgment and the gospel. In Scripture, judgment is an integral part of the good news of the gospel. Judgment results in the vindication and release of God's people; it also results in the punishment of the wicked. The gospel includes both aspects of judgment.

We first see this linkage in the Garden of Eden. After Adam and Eve sinned, God came in judgment. The first act of judgment God did was to punish the serpent. The second was to release from Satan's control those whom he had made his captives. In the first announcement of the gospel, Genesis 3:15, the two phases of judgment were linked together.

The great Flood provides another example of the link between judgment and salvation. God sent a massive catastrophe to destroy the wicked and re-shape the surface of the earth, but "Noah found grace in the eyes of the Lord" (Genesis 6:8). At the end of the Flood, a special blessing was pronounced on Noah and his family: "God blessed Noah and his sons, and said to them: 'Be fruitful and multiply, and fill the earth' " (Genesis 9:1). This blessing is similar to the one given to Adam and Eve right after they were created (Genesis 1:28). After evil had been dealt with, Noah was given freedom and a blessing.

A third example of the combination of punishment of the wicked and reward of God's people is seen in the end-time prophecies of deliverance of God's people. Daniel wrote, "There shall be a time of trouble, such as never was since there was a nation, even to that time. And at that time your people shall be delivered, every one who is found written in the book" (Daniel 12:1).

Revelation presents that same theme. First, the guilty are punished, this time in the seven last plagues (Revelation 16–18), and then the righteous are rescued (Revelation 21; 22). And the judgment that brings punishment to the wicked also brings the salvation of God's people.

Jesus' teaching had a similar pattern: " 'I tell you, in that night there will be two men in one bed: the one will be taken and the other will be left. Two women will be grinding together: the one will be taken and the other left.' . . . And they answered and said to Him, 'Where, Lord?' So He said to them, 'Wherever the body is, there the eagles will be gathered together' " (Luke 17:34–37).

First, some are taken for destruction. Then those who remain will be gathered into the kingdom.

This is further explained in the parable of the tares: " 'Let both grow together until the harvest, and at the time of the harvest I will say to the reapers, "First gather together the tares and bind them in bundles to burn them, but gather the wheat into my barn" ' " (Matthew 13:30).

These examples explain the link between the gospel and judgment as seen in the first angel's message.

Creation, judgment, and the gospel. The gospel is intimately linked to Creation. Only someone with absolute power over all of creation could carry out both aspects of judgment—overcoming the devil and bringing freedom to God's people.

Only the Creator could bring a curse on the serpent in Eden and extend the lives of Adam and Eve.

Only the Creator could bring a global Flood that tore up the entire crust of the earth and destroyed all land animals outside the ark while He protected Noah and his family and the ark during that terrible catastrophe.

Only the Creator has the power over nature seen in the life and ministry of Jesus Christ. Only the Creator could restore diseased tissues and create new pathways in the brain, enabling the lame to walk and the blind to see. Only the Creator could lay down His life voluntarily and take it up again.

Only the Creator has the power to bring earth's history to a climax through upheavals of nature.

Only the Creator has the power to create a new heavens and a new earth.

Only the Creator can overthrow the powers of evil and bring salvation to God's people.

Without Creation and the Creator, there can be no gospel.

The parallel between Creation and judgment in the first angel's message is clear. The power and goodness of the Creator are the basis of our confidence in the power of the Judge both to end sin and to create a new world in righteousness (2 Peter 3:13).

Creation makes a difference for the gospel

The truth of the biblical story of Creation establishes the logic of the gospel and assures its eventual success. Alternative, man-made stories that deny the six-day Creation of Genesis don't provide support for either the logic of the gospel or the assurance of its fulfillment.

The Creation story is the logical foundation for the gospel because the good news of salvation through Jesus Christ is logically predicated on the fact that humans were created better than we are now. We have fallen from our original state, not risen from the beasts. Otherwise, why would we need to be saved, and from what?

Evolutionary theory teaches that death is not caused by sin, but is part of the essence of nature. Evolution cannot function without death, and on the other hand, the ultimate goal of Christianity—the gospel—is victory over death so that we can live with God forever. Where is the basis for the gospel in evolutionary thought? It isn't there. It is the biblical story of Creation and the Fall that explains the need and purpose of the gospel.

The Creation story is also the basis for our assurance of salvation. The salvation of humans is based on the special status God gave to them at Creation. The power of the Creator in transforming the dust into a living person provides a precedent for the transformation that must take place at the resurrection. Evolutionary thought provides no such confidence. Where is the basis for a supernatural resurrection into a sinless and death-less state if the only precedent we have is gradual development over eons of time via the death of millions of intermediate forms? There isn't any. It is the biblical story of Creation in six days that gives us assurance that God will re-create us in perfection "in a moment" (1 Corinthians 15:52).

Conclusion

The gospel of salvation through the life, death, and resurrection of Jesus Christ is intimately and logically linked to the biblical story of Creation in six literal days. Humans enjoy a special relationship with God because only they were created in His image. Death is an enemy to both God and humans; it is not an essential part of nature. The outcome of the gospel is the restoration of humans to the special status with which they were originally created. No other theory of origins provides the logical basis for the gospel, explains our need for salvation, or gives us assurance of its success.

---

1. See Ojewole, A. *The Seed in Genesis 3:15: An Exegetical and Intertextual Study.* ATS Monograph Series. Berrien Springs, MI: Adventist Theological Society Publications (2011).

2. Malachi 4:1 indicates that the wicked will be destroyed, root (Satan) and branch (his followers); cf. Revelation 20:9, 10. In verse 10, the phrase "forever and ever" does not necessarily mean of infinite duration, but of an indefinite, extended duration.

3. Cf. 2 Thessalonians 4:16, 17; Revelation 20:4–6.

4. Paulien, J. *Seven Keys: Unlocking the Secrets of Revelation.* Nampa, ID: Pacific Press® (2009).

CHAPTER 13

Creation and Our View of Life

Two people may see the same thing but draw completely different conclusions about it. For example, the psalmist wrote, "The heavens declare the glory of God; and the firmament shows His handiwork" (Psalm 19:1). In contrast, Steven Weinberg, winner of the 1979 Nobel Prize in physics, wrote, "The stars tell us nothing more or less about the glory of God than do the stones on the ground around us."[1] How can two people come to such contrasting conclusions from the same observation?

The answer lies in the different viewpoints of those people—in what is known as a worldview.[2] Each of us has a worldview, although most of us may never have thought about it. By understanding the nature of worldviews and the ways in which they differ, we can understand better why people have such different convictions about life and truth. In the process, we will discover that one's view of origins has a very strong effect on one's understanding of reality.

A worldview is a set of assumptions that we accept, often subconsciously, about the structure and meaning of the world.[3] It includes assumptions we make about ourselves, the world, and God. A worldview is constructed from one's beliefs about ourselves and our world—beliefs that answer the following questions:

1. What is the basis of reality? Is it God, matter, or both?
2. What is my place in the universe, both now and in the future? Is there a purpose for my existence? What happens when I die?
3. How should I behave, and why should I behave that way? Is there a standard of morality? Does it matter?
4. What has made the world what it is today? Is there a plan, or is its state a matter of chance or fate?
5. How can I know what is true? Is some truth beyond my ability to sense or to understand?

People's answers to these questions differ, which explains why there are different worldviews.

Three basic categories

Most worldviews can be classified as belonging within one of three categories: theism, materialism, or pantheism.[4]

Biblical theism. People whose worldview is biblical theism believe in the existence of a single, supreme Creator God who has revealed Himself to humans through the Bible. Basic to this worldview is the conviction that God inspired the writing of the Bible, which is His truthful revelation of Himself to humans. From this basis, biblical theism offers the following responses to the worldview questions listed above.

1. What is the basis of reality?

God is the Source and Basis of reality. He is omnipotent, omniscient, omnipresent, eternal, infinite, personal, and good. The universe is a creation. It is orderly and good and is sustained by a God who is consistent and yet is open to performing unique acts—He does perform miracles.

2. What is my place in the universe?

God created humans in His image, but they rebelled, distorting that image and becoming evil. God devised a plan whereby humans could be restored to fellowship with Him through the life, death, and resurrection of Jesus Christ. Death is a temporary sleeplike state that will be interrupted by resurrection and then followed either by eternal life or eternal extinction. Human existence has meaning because God values humans and has provided a means of restoring them to their original state through the life, death, and resurrection of Jesus Christ.

3. How should I behave, and why?

Humans should live in harmony with God's Word. God is good, and He loves us, so His instructions are wise and in our best interest. Rejection of God's principles produces evil, which, in turn, produces destructive results. Humans are in a state of rebellion, but God has provided a means of restoration and the eventual elimination of evil, while preserving freedom of choice.

4. What has made the world what it is today?

Originally, creation was very good because it was made by a good God. It was beautiful and harmonious, and there was no violence, suffering, or death. It became corrupted when humans rebelled against God and gave Satan the opportunity to bring evil into the world. Satan is a personal being committed to rebellion against God. He is the original source of evil.

5. How can I know what is true?

Truth comes from God, who reveals it to humans primarily through the Bible and the guidance of the Holy Spirit, but also through providence, experience, and design in nature.

Materialism. Those who hold this worldview believe that matter is all that exists and that the universe is governed by chance and natural law. They don't believe there is a spiritual realm. The materialistic worldview provides the following responses to the five worldview questions.

1. What is the basis of reality?

Matter is all that exists—there are no gods. The universe is governed only by chance and inherent properties known as natural laws. It isn't influenced by anything outside of the universe. Miracles do not occur.

2. What is my place in the universe?

Humans are complex "biorobots" consisting of physical properties and chemical reactions with no extrinsic purpose or intrinsic value. Free will is an illusion. Death is molecular disassembly and extinction, and there is no future life.

3. How should I behave, and why?

Laws govern the physical universe, but there is no absolute standard of morality. Good and evil are simply labels for the behaviors we like and those we don't, and our tastes and values change over time.

4. What has made the world what it is today?

The laws of nature are such that some favorable events occur and some unfavorable events occur—it's all a matter of chance and natural law.

5. How can I know what is true?

Knowledge comes from experience and is relative. Absolute truth is unknowable.

Pantheism. The foundational belief of this worldview is that God and nature are the same. Pantheism's view of reality varies. Some hold that all reality is matter; some that all is spirit; and some a mixture of these two ideas. Pantheism is highly plastic, as is seen in the differing forms it assumes in Taoism, Hinduism, Buddhism, animism, and other religions and philosophies. This worldview typically includes a fear of or religious reverence for nature. Though the different forms of pantheism vary considerably, the following responses to our five basic questions are typical of this worldview.

1. What is the basis of reality?

The universe is spirit. There is no personal God. Instead, there is a universal, impersonal spirit present in all matter. All things share this universal spirit and strive to achieve unity with it.

2. What is my place in the universe?

Humans are evolving toward divinity and union with the universal spirit. Death ends one's personhood but doesn't change one's relationship with the spirit. To become one with the universe is to pass beyond personality and time and to re-enter the cycle of history.

3. How should I behave, and why?

There is no right or wrong. Though all of us walk on different paths, we're all evolving toward unity. We should act in harmony with nature and aim to become one with the universal spirit. The measure of how good a life we're living is how happy we are.

4. What has made the world what it is today?

Pantheism is not concerned with good and evil. Those notions are merely different manifestations of the universal spirit expressed in different ways. All things are striving for unity through evolution of the spirit.

5. How can I know what is true?

Whether something is true or false isn't important. To become one with the universe is to pass beyond knowledge, where there is no such thing as contradiction.

Origins and worldviews

One's view of origins directly influences one's worldview and shapes one's relationship to God, to other humans, and to the world in general. Neither materialism nor pantheism provides satisfactory explanations for the origin of the universe or for the presence of good and evil in the world. Belief in origin by direct creation leads directly to belief in an active, personal God who created humans in His image, who cares about His creation, and who has provided moral instruction on how to relate to the rest of creation. And conversely, rejection of biblical creation leads to views of God, humans, and nature that are inconsistent with biblical theism. Belief in origin by naturalistic evolution leads one toward belief that there is no God, no purpose for nature or for human life, and no moral absolutes. And belief in origin by spirit-guided evolution inclines one toward belief in pantheism, the upward progress of humanity, and moral relativism. Neither of these worldviews is consistent with the idea that humans were specially created and are in need of salvation.

The biblical Creation story includes three crucial points that have important implications for the character of the Creator: God created by fiat in six days; the creation of humans differed from that of the other creatures; and originally, what God created was good, but it has been corrupted by sin. These three points help shape the Adventist worldview.

First, Creation by fiat in six days implies that God created without violence, suffering, or death. He is in control of the creation and is not in any way restricted by "natural laws," time, or process. The days of Creation set a pattern for establishing the length of the week and thus for identifying the seventh-day Sabbath. Denial of Creation by fiat in six days undermines the logical basis of each of these parts of the Adventist worldview.

Second, the special creation of humans implies that God, in person, created them in His image, and that originally they were without fault. Humans are holistic and mortal. They are neither embodied immortal spirits nor fortuitous collections of molecules. Humans differ qualitatively from ordinary animals. Denial of the special creation of humans undermines each of these points.

Third, belief in a good creation that sin has corrupted implies that the Creator was good. Death, suffering, and violence came into the world after Creation. They were the result of Adam's disobedience, which gave Satan full access to this world. The present condition of the creation is neither original nor normative. Denial of a good creation corrupted by sin undermines each of these points. Note the contradictions between these points and all theories that propose that humans evolved upward from animals.

The "great controversy." The major elements of biblical theism have been grouped into an explanatory story known as the great controversy. The story goes something like this: A good God created intelligent beings with freedom of choice. God appointed one of these beings, one named Lucifer, to a position close to God Himself. Lucifer became proud of his beauty and intelligence, and he rebelled and thus became Satan, the enemy of God.

God had been planning to create our world, and despite the complication posed by Lucifer, He carried out His plan. That included creating Adam and Eve, the first humans, in His own image and giving them the responsibility of governing the world.

However, Satan deceived Adam and Eve, leading them into rebellion against God and thereby gaining full access to this world. But God promised the first couple that Satan would eventually be defeated. Jesus Christ accomplished this, living on earth, dying in our place so He could save us without sacrificing justice (Romans 3:21–26), and rising to life again, thus defeating the devil. Eventually, Jesus will resurrect those who have accepted His grace, and He will destroy Satan and his followers and then will give His people a re-created, flawless new earth in which they will live with Him eternally.

Creation and re-creation. The biblical promise of a new creation (Revelation 21:1)[5] is linked in several important ways with the first creation. In neither case is a tabernacle, sanctuary, or temple needed. The whole Garden was a temple, and so will the New Jerusalem be (Revelation 22:3). In both settings, God and humans communicate face to face (Genesis 2:15–19; Revelation 22:4). The tree of life, once in Eden, will be present in the new earth (Revelation 22:2). And, as in Eden, there is no suffering, violence, or predation in the new earth (Genesis 1:30; Revelation 21:4). That place is lighted by the presence of God—which may have been the case during the first three days of Creation, after God divided the light from the darkness but before He appointed the sun to its task (Genesis 1:4, 14–16; Revelation 21:23). The reality of the first creation is the guarantee of a new creation. Both are integral parts of the biblical worldview.

Creation and worldview

Biblical Creation is vitally linked with the basic elements of Christianity—the moral nature of humans, the origin of evil, the nature and meaning of marriage, our role as stewards of the world, the Sabbath, and, most important, the gospel. Despite this linkage, many Christians are troubled by the failure of science to confirm the biblical story. For some, the idea that God used an evolutionary process as His chosen method for creation seems a way to keep both God and science in the picture.

However, whether called theistic evolution or evolutionary creation, the idea that evolution is God's chosen method of creation is neither good science nor good theology. It isn't good science because it posits forces that are, in principle, undetectable, untestable, and *ad hoc*. If one wishes to postulate an invisible, undetectable force, it makes little difference scientifically whether one calls that force God, a fairy, or an earth-spirit. Science has no place for such ideas.

The idea that God chose evolutionary processes as His method of creation is not good theology either. There is no basis in Scripture for such an idea. It implies a "god" of death and evil who was either unable or unwilling to create humans the way he wanted them to be. He had to use a process based on death to develop humans into what he wanted them to be. The theory also implies that this god requires humans to be morally better than he is—he expects them to treat the weak better than he did in the evolutionary process he used to fill the earth. It implies that modern humans are better able to discover what God is like than those to whom God revealed Himself in the past. It values current human opinion more than it does the teachings of Scripture. People tend to pattern their behavior after that of their god(s). That's unfortunate, for their gods are poor examples, and religion compatible with evolution is powerless—it does nothing to help people deal with sin.

Several important practical implications for religious life can be inferred from evolutionary creation. First, it seems pointless to pray to a deity who was unable (or unwilling) to accomplish directly what he wanted. Second, it is questionable whether one can trust a deity who condemns those he has created for treating the weak in the same way that he treated them. Third, by rejecting the authority of Scripture, it removes the basis for any objective standard of morality or hope of miraculous resurrection.

Three other implications of evolutionary creation should cause us to stop and think carefully. The first is one we've pointed out previously: its negation of the six-day Creation and seventh-day Sabbath. A second startling implication of evolutionary creation or theistic evolution is its failure to distinguish between humans and other animals. If humans descended from nonhumans, how do they differ from other animals? The most common explanation is that God planted immortal souls in some animals, transforming them into morally accountable human beings. Adoption of the theory of evolutionary creation leads easily and logically to the twin errors of Sunday observance and immortality of the soul. This combination has the potential to support the formation of a false religion and eventually to establish religious intolerance and persecution.[6]

The final implication of evolutionary creation may be the most serious—it opposes the gospel. If humans are the product of an evolutionary progression, they have never been better than they are at the present time. As one author wrote, if there was a fall, it was a "fall upward."[7] But there is no "fall" in evolutionary theory, no curse on nature, and no relationship between sin and death. Rather, death is an integral part of nature, suffering has always existed, and the state of nature is the same today as it has always been. If one grants these points to be true, there is no Paradise to restore, no tree of life or of knowledge, and no evil to overcome. So, a new "gospel" must be invented.[8] Exactly what this gospel might be depends on the person who invents it, but it cannot logically be the gospel of restoration preached by the apostle Paul (Romans 8:20, 21).

Conclusion

The biblical worldview begins with the literal Creation story in Genesis. This story provides the backdrop against which the elements of the biblical worldview acquire their meaning. Theories that mix elements from different worldviews suffer from faulty logic. And theories that picture humans evolving from animals don't fit with the biblical story of sin and salvation and should be rejected by Christians. In many ways—including our understanding of the character of God, the relationship of humans to the rest of the creation, and the nature, meaning, and destiny of human life—biblical Creation makes an important difference.

---

1. Weinberg, S. *Dreams of a Final Theory*. New York: Vintage Books (1992), 241.

2. The term is derived from the German *Weltanschauung,* meaning "worldview."

3. A good introduction to this topic from a Christian perspective is: Sire, JW. *The Universe Next Door*. Downers Grove, IL: IVP Academic (2009).

4. See Rasi, H. "Why Do Different Scientists Interpret Reality Differently?" in Gibson, LJ. and HR. Rasi, eds. *Understanding Creation*. Nampa, ID: Pacific Press® (2011), 11–24.

5. Cf. 2 Peter 3:13; Isaiah 65:17.

6. White, EG. *The Great Controversy*. Nampa, ID: Pacific Press® (2005), 588.

7. "We appear to be rising beasts rather than fallen angels." Peacocke, A. "Biology and a Theology of Evolution," *Zygon* 34/4:695–712 (1999). Some Mormons use that term to mean that Adam's fall brought good in that it resulted in reproduction and the filling of the earth.

8. Paul condemned such efforts; see Galatians 1:6–9.

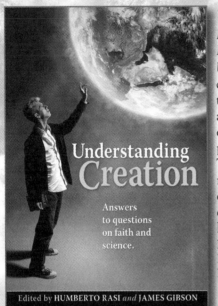